THE MANIFEST PRESENCE OF GOD

My Spiritual Journey

WALTER BEUTTLER

EDITED BY WADE TAYLOR

The Manifest Presence of God

Edited by Wade E Taylor
Parousia Ministries

COPYRIGHT © 2008
2nd edition © 2015
This copyright applies to these edited editions only

This book may be reproduced for personal edification and study so long as not used for financial gain.

Any posting of this book on another web site is forbidden.

Scripture quotations are from the King James Easy Reading Study Bible, unless otherwise indicated. Copyright © 2002 G.E.M. Publishing.

In the King James Easy Reading Study Bible, archaic forms are replaced with current usage. Otherwise, it is a word for word rendering of the King James text.

Scripture quotations marked ASV are taken from the American Standard Version of the Bible and those marked NAS are taken from the New American Standard Bible; Copyright © by The Lockman Foundation; used by permission.

This book is dedicated to the glory and adoration of God and to all who desire a closer walk with Him.

TABLE OF CONTENTS

Preface Wade Taylor vii

Introduction ix

Chapter 1 The Importance of the Manifest
          Presence of God 1

Chapter 2 The Error of Uzzah 7

Chapter 3 Divine Appointments 13

Chapter 4 Face to Face 21

Chapter 5 Glory about Him 27

Chapter 6 God's Deep Secrets 35

Chapter 7 Knowledge of God 43

Chapter 8 The Manifest Presence of God 49

Chapter 9 Spiritual Sensitivity 55

Chapter 10 Manifestations of the Divine Presence 63

Chapter 11 Quickening Presence 71

Chapter 12 When He calls I will Answer 79

Chapter 13 A Hearing Heart 85

Chapter 14 Those That Seek Me Early Shall Find Me 91

Chapter 15 To Him that Overcomes 99

Chapter 16 **Bonus Message 1** Laws Governing
                the Presence..107

Chapter 17 **Bonus Message 2** Four Ways to
                Lose God's Presence 131

Afterword..157

Preface

Wade E Taylor

Walter Beuttler was a teacher in the Bible School that I attended. He personally knew and walked with the Lord as few have.

I personally witnessed the effect and the outworking of the very unusual personal relationship which he maintained with the Lord. The Lord often visited the classroom, as he taught, to reveal Himself and manifestly move in the lives of the students who sat under his ministry. As a result, my life was both challenged and changed.

He often exhorted his students to cultivate a personal, experiential knowledge of the Lord. He used his unique spiritual walk and experiences with the Lord as a means to provoke us to begin seeking the Lord in earnest.

Through his ministry, two aspects of my spiritual life became very important. The first was my newfound understanding of the immeasurable benefit of spending quality time *"waiting upon the Lord."* The second was my coming to know that it is possible to experience the

"*Manifest Presence*" of the Lord. Through his ministry, these became a reality in my life.

A spiritual principle that Walter Beuttler imparted through his classroom teaching greatly affected my spiritual life, and became a foundational principle in my ministry.

> "*If we build God a house of devotion,*
>
> *He will build us a house of ministry.*"

I can truly testify that this principle works.

Walter Beuttler traveled extensively in overseas ministry, teaching the principles of the "*Manifest Presence of the Lord,*" and "*Divine Guidance,*" until close to the time of his death in 1974.

Introduction

My Memories of Walter Beuttler and his dear wife Elizabeth Beuttler

Introduction by Bill Burkett

When I attended EBI, Green Lane, Pennsylvania, I had just months previously been discharged from the USAF after serving in the Korean theatre. I had married a year before my discharge and upon returning I found the Lord at the Bethel Temple Assembly of God church in Sacramento, California under Nelson Hinman. It was Sunday morning service, February 18, 1951. I had been saved about two years when I entered EBI on my GI Bill of Rights. To this day I praise God for leading me to choose EBI for my bible training. It was there a select group of very godly men and several lady teachers had been brought together. Walter Beuttler was one of those choice servants.

I sat under brother Beuttler's classroom teaching for two years always relishing the things I would hear him share in class. Many years have gone by since those days and a part of him remains in me as in the life of most of the students who had the privilege of sitting under his teaching. He instilled in every student the great essential of having an intimate relationship with God. He taught us how wait on the Lord and give that pursuit a very high priority in our lives as minister's of His Word. We often experienced first-hand exactly what he was teaching us when the Holy Spirit would suddenly fall over the classroom with his wondrous sense of presence. "Student's close your books, he is here." Quietly we would close our books and slip our notes inside out Bibles. Then we would start waiting and breathing in the presence of the Holy Spirit. A message in another language would be heard and a word of interpretation would follow giving the class direction or admonishing us. The rest of the class period was given to praying and several others could be heard weeping as the Holy Spirit was doing His work secretly in the heart of each student. When we drew near the end of the class period brother Beuttler would softly lead out with prayer. When we came to the end of the visitation of the Lord's special presence, brother Beuttler would smile at us and say, "Isn't He nice?"

I returned to campus for several years after my last year, always making contact with him. I had become full time as a missionary evangelist and he always had time to spend with me. I was privileged to become his friend, to visit his home and eat sister Beuttler's delicious dinners. I was probably one of the few he ever took to his attic tryst where he spent hours if not days alone with God. I remember the first time he invited me to follow him to his meeting place. It was after a meal and when we rose from the table he said to me; Come with me, brother Burkett. We walked into another room and he opened a door and started up a narrow stairway. As I followed him I had the feeling I was experiencing something special but not sure what. He took me to the attic room of the house he had finished off for his place to meet with the Lord. I was awed to think he allowed me to be in that room. The steps and floors were carpeted to make the acoustics low. In the center of the big attic room was a reclining chair and a table on either side. Both were laden with books and study notes. This was long before computers when we did all of our studying of the word surrounded by the Bible and reference books. The walls held shelves of his books, his collection over the years of a very carefully selected personal library. I had a very humble feeling that he was sharing with me a very sacred part of his life. At that visit in the early 70's he was already battling a terminal disease but never mentioned it to me. After brother Beuttler departed this life I visited sister Beuttler a couple of times when she was living alone. I also remember meeting at that time his daughter and son-in-law, pastor White. I remember on one of those visits sister Beuttler took me to a file cabinet and shared with me his collection of notes. He had compiled a very nicely printed set of his classroom notes in a red NorthEast notebook. At that time sister Beuttler gave me permission use and reprint his notes in any way I would care to. Since then I have shared them far and wide and they now appear on this website for all. She gave me several of the red notebooks of his complete set of notes. One of the first men I shared one of his notebooks with was Jim Cymbala, pastor of the Brooklyn Tabernacle.

In closing I would like to say that I have so many precious memories of my many talks with brother Beuttler and the things that went on in his classes and the chapel services. He always sat in the front row of the chapel on the left side which was the girls seating side of the chapel. You always had the feeling that brother Beuttler was monitoring the direction of the service along with brother Wells, president of the Bible School who sat on the boys side of the chapel seating. If someone would start singing the wrong chorus when the Holy Spirit wanted quietness and listening for His leading, brother Beuttler had a way of getting it back on track and into the hands of the Holy Spirit again. My first year, 1951, was the year after EBI had experienced a tremendous revival that marked by visions and miracles. All of my first year I sat spellbound listening often to students who witnessed and took part in that revival. But in 1951 we also had wonderful visitations that shut down classes as we sat in chapel and waited in his presence, praying and confessing sins. Brother Beuttler was always there worshipping with us but he never did anything to lead. He was very careful to allow only the Holy Spirit to lead the meetings through the gifts and waves of God's presence. Brother Bongiarno sat beside me in chapel one morning when suddenly the gush of cool Autumn wind came through the windows carrying the fragrance of an orange orchard in full blossom! It filled the chapel as we breathed in the fragrance of the Holy Spirit. I still praise God for the glorious truths and wonders of the Spirit I learned then as a young man.

The Manifest Presence of God

A little bit on the humorous side; I like bow ties and even though brother Beuttler never saw me wear one, I often wore bow ties but not on campus at EBI. One day in class he said in a rather critical tone, "Bow ties are propellers," in his German accent. I never wore one again while attending EBI.

There are two things that is seldom mentioned about his person: The first is his German accent that was so much a part of his personality. He told us many stories about the funny things he went through learning English when he first came to the States. In one class he was teaching on the attributes of God and I was always full of questions. In that particular class I had my hand up all the time, thinking so deeply that I didn't realize how much I was interrupting his thoughts. After answering my question (what part do angels have in the omnipresence of God?) I knew he was a little annoyed with me when he raise his pencil with both hands and rolled the pencil with his fingers glaring over it at me and said, "One fool can ask more questions than ten wise men can answer." It must have been a German proverb – but I got the message and woke up to my inconsideration.

Another thing that was peculiar about brother Beuttler's classes was his 5 question test on a small 5" x 4" piece of paper at the beginning of each class on the material covered in the previous class. The book store carried "Beuttler pads" for his classes. Many years later I lived in China seven years teaching linguistics to English majors in several different universities. I used that method of testing to keep my student's noses to the grindstone! It was very effective and I made it 20% of the grade value.

I suppose I could write a small book about brother Beuttler but I have tried to write some things here that will make those who want to know more about this man of God in a more personal way. I am 84 at this writing and still remember vividly my many experiences under Walter Beuttler.

Bill Burkett.

http://actsion.com/walter-beuttlers-bible-study-notes/

Chapter 1

The Importance of the Manifest Presence of God

Several years ago, the Lord asked me to shut myself in with Him. I found a place where I could be totally alone with the Lord in fasting and prayer.

Sunday afternoon, I realized that I had spent 48 hours in prayer, fasting, and seeking the Lord, with no results. I had neither felt nor received anything, nor was I aware of His presence. I knew the Lord wanted to speak, but He did not do so.

Then I said within my heart, "*It takes God a long time to speak.*" No sooner had I said this, than the Lord spoke to me in a voice that was as clear as a bell, and as sharp as a razor. This was a voice which was not audible, but a voice that I heard. He said, "*To hurry God is to find fault with Him.*"

The Lord said I was criticizing Him because I thought He was too slow. I apologized and asked Him to forgive me.

As soon as I did this, the Lord walked through the door into the room where I had been waiting upon Him. I did not see or hear Him, but it was so real that sight could not have made it any more real. The Lord walked in, and His presence followed behind Him, which was as a Royal Dignitary walking to His Throne with a long robe following, which spread throughout the entire room.

The Lord came and stood to my left, approximately an arm's length away, and He stayed there for four hours. During this time, He taught me from His Word on the subject of *"Knowing God."* I was given a Scripture, which I found and read. Then it would marvelously unfold so I could see its beauty, depth, and purpose.

The next summer, I was in Bangkok, Thailand. As I walked along the street, I saw a lotus bud lying on the side of the road. I picked it up, pulled the petals back and delighted myself at the beautiful arrangement of the lotus within. This was as the Lord did, as He marvelously unfolded His Word in all its beauty and fullness. Our knowing Him is very near to the heart of God. This is a *"knowing"* that includes the knowledge and personal experience of the *"manifest presence of God."*

At six o‹clock, the Lord turned, faced the door, and said, *"And the Lord left him to try him."* With that, His presence collected from all over the room, and followed Him as He left.

These four hours of *"personal teaching"* from a *"personal Christ"* on the *"true knowledge of God"* were beyond anything I could have anticipated. I did not know that later He would send me into more than one hundred countries to share what I had learned during that time.

In sharing the experience that followed this visitation from the Lord, I am very carefully choosing each word. This is the absolute unembroidered truth, recounted as accurately as I know how.

The Lord had said that He "*left him to try him.*" In school, we teach, and then give a test. I thought that since the Lord had been teaching me, He would test me on what I had learned. I waited, but nothing happened, so I thought I would go to bed. It was only eight o'clock, but I had slept very little since Friday.

Then Satan walked through the door into the room, as if the door had not been there. I was standing by the bed and recognized him at once. He entered precisely as the Lord had entered, and stood where the Lord had stood. Behind him followed a satanic presence, like a regal robe of some sovereign, which spread throughout the entire room exactly as the Lord's presence had done. I was not aware that I had any fear as Satan spoke. His voice was not audible, yet it was a clear distinct voice that I heard.

He said, "*The Lord did not visit you.*" I answered out loud, "*Yes, He did.*" Next, he said, "*The Bible is not the Word of God.*" I responded, "*Yes it is.*" Then he said, "*The Lord did not teach you,*" and I replied, "*Yes He did.*" Following this exchange, he said, "*Why don't you deny God?*" I said, "*Why should I?*" He responded, "*Because God is not a real God,*" and I said, "*I know He is real.*" Then he said, "*You are not saved,*" and I said, "*I know that I am saved.*"

After this, he said, "*You are praying too much,*" and I said, "*No, I am not.*" Then even stronger, he said, "*You will lose your mind because you are praying too much,*" and I answered, "*I am not praying too much, and I will not lose my mind.*"

This went on for some time while I stood by the bed. Then it seemed as if the room began to turn, and I was in the center of a merry-go-round that went faster and faster. Then he said, "*See, you are losing your mind.*" I said, "*No, this is only an illusion, nothing is moving. You are trying to deceive me and make me think the room is moving when it is not.*"

This was a very serious matter, as I began to see triangles, circles, squares, trees, rocks, and mountains, as everything moved around in the room. Then he again said, "*Are you ready to deny God,*" and I said, "*No, I will never be ready.*"

I firmly held my ground as he attempted to cause me to deny all that the Lord had taught me. Then he turned and went out through the door. As he did, the whole satanic presence collected, and followed him like a regal robe out of the room, and I was again with the Lord.

I noticed that it was now ten o'clock, and thought I would now go to bed. Then Satan walked in the second time and stood where he had been, and again his presence followed him and filled the room. This time, everything seemed to be much stronger. We went through the whole thing again with one difference; there was a tremendous power that came from him. When he spoke, *"Are you ready to give up?"* It came with an authority that was frightening.

I noticed that I was weakening. I could tell that my answers were no longer as resolute as they had been. He kept hammering away to cause me to give in, and I resisted until I had no more will to resist. Finally, I said within myself, *"I can resist no longer,"* and threw myself on the bed, seemingly in defeat.

Just as I struck the bed, I felt something stir within me. I knew it was the presence of the Holy Spirit. I now concentrated on this presence that was inside of me. Satan was still there, but I ignored him and concentrated on this presence of the Lord. As I did this, the presence began to slowly expand and sing. It was not me that sang, but the Holy Spirit within me. I clearly heard Him sing the chorus, *"Isn't He wonderful, wonderful, wonderful, isn't Jesus my Lord wonderful."*

As the Holy Spirit continued to sing, His presence became larger and stronger. I listened, and presumably the devil listened also, but said nothing. I was occupied with what was going on inside of me. Finally, His presence reached my throat and I joined in and sang with Him. Satan still had nothing to say, as I sang out loud while the Holy Spirit sang within me.

Then the Holy Spirit stopped, and I waited. He (*the Holy Spirit*) spoke and said, *"When the enemy shall come in like a flood, then the Spirit shall raise an arm in defense against him*" (Isaiah 59:18). With that, Satan turned and quickly left, and the glory of the Lord filled the entire room. The Holy Spirit came to my defense at the very moment I had become too weak to resist. Now it was midnight. The next day, I returned home.

You may wonder, why did this happen? For four hours, the Lord had been teaching me things about the knowledge of God, and about His personalized manifest presence. The enemy sought to destroy the very thing the Lord had given me. The one thing the devil hates is for us to personally know God. He does not want the Lord's people to experience the *"personal manifest presence of God"* in their lives.

I believe the reason the devil tried so hard to defeat me is due to the vital importance of this message concerning our *"personally knowing the Lord,"* and the *"reality of His manifest presence."*

Chapter 2

The Error of Uzzah

Note: During 1951, a revival was experienced in the Bible School where Walter Beuttler taught. The Lord used this move of the Spirit to put into operation the things He had taught him during an intense visitation while in a motel room. Brother Beuttler had drawn aside to meet the Lord, Who in turn manifested His glory to him. This manifestation was immediately challenged by Satan. The following is Brother Beuttler›s account of some of the Lord's dealings in the outworking of his calling to a ministry to the nations, which came during his personal visitation with the Lord.

During this revival, the Lord awakened me each morning at three o'clock. This meant I stayed up the rest of the night, sitting in His presence so I would be ready for the services. During this time, the Lord gave the outline for the services during that day.

During a Friday night service, there was a mighty move of the Holy Spirit, and some of the students seemed to be going beyond what the Holy Spirit was doing. Because I was in charge, I put my hands on the fellows who were having these manifestations, which to me, seemed so out of place. In restraining them, I did so in a wrong spirit, as a reaction to what was happening. As soon as I did this, the moving of the Spirit stopped and I knew I had killed the meeting. It was as though a blight struck the meeting - it was finished. I dismissed the service and went home.

That night, at two-thirty, while still asleep, I was awakened by a man's voice singing audibly in my bedroom. I looked in the direction of the voice, and I saw the Lord standing there. He was dressed in white garments, looking toward me, as He sang. I heard Him like I hear a man's voice, and I saw Him, as I would see you. This has happened only once in my life.

I sat up in bed as He sang two stanzas. Apparently I was awakened just as He began the first stanza, which had to do with sin and forgiveness. After this, I went to my chair and sat there, waiting before the Lord. There was an unusual presence of the Lord, as I mused over the song that He sang.

I was considering the second stanza, and seemed to push away the thought of the first stanza, which had to do with sin.

When I realized what I was doing, I said, *"Lord is something wrong?"* I heard the answer right away, *"The error of Uzzah."*

In the Old Testament, Uzzah had touched the ark of God and died. The Lord was saying, *"You committed the same* sin as Uzzah; you touched the ark of God." I did not die because Jesus had died in my place two thousand years before, but it was sin nevertheless. I said, "*Lord I am sorry, I did not mean to stop the moving of the Holy Spirit.*" The Lord knew that, but neither did Uzzah intend to stop the progress of the ark.

I told the Lord that I did not know what I should do. At once I received the answer; "*On Sunday morning, during the communion service, you are to make a public confession to the whole student body for what you did, and ask the students forgiveness.*" I squirmed when I heard this. I knew He meant it, and that there was no way out. I said, "*Lord, I do not know how I can do a humbling thing like that, but I will do it.*"

Sunday morning came, and as the bread was distributed, my heart suddenly began to pound so hard I thought it would jump out. I knew this was the signal to obey what the Lord had told me. I stood up and said, "*Students, I have a confession to make.*" You could have heard a pin drop in the silence. And I could hear their thoughts, "*Brother Beuttler, confess?*" I told them exactly what had happened and said, "*I ask your forgiveness.*"

As soon as I finished, one of the students gave a powerful utterance in prophecy. "*Because you have done this thing,* (*it was obviously addressed to me*), *and have humbled yourself in the sight of this congregation, the Lord your God will lift you above your fellows and make of you a city set on a hill.*"

When I heard this, I dropped between the seats and wept.

As I did, the Lord spoke to me saying, *"Go and teach all nations."* If I had not humbled myself that morning, I do not believe God would have sent me around the world to carry the truths that Jesus taught me, and which Satan had challenged, while seeking the Lord in the motel room.

Teach all nations? Where would I go, and on what? Bible School teachers did not receive salaries, especially in those days. We were as *"poor as a church mouse."* A few weeks later, the Lord spoke, *"Get a passport."* I thought, *"Lord, I have no money to go anywhere."* Later, the Lord again said, *"Get a passport."* I thought, *"How could I go?"*

Then after several days, the Lord spoke a third time. This was strong and clear, *"Get a passport."* I hesitated again and said, *"Lord, why spend money for a passport, I cannot go anywhere."* About two weeks later after speaking at a church, a lady said, *"I have an airplane ticket to go to Europe and I cannot go. I felt I was to give it to you. Do you have a passport?"*

I said, *"I will get one right away."* She responded, *"It takes four weeks to get a passport, and this flight leaves in two weeks."* I stayed home, keenly feeling my disobedience to the Lord.

The Lord said nothing about traveling for the next nine months. I would say, *"Lord, when am I to go?"* There was no response, but I did get my passport. Then I felt it was the time to go, and began to look for someone to give me a ticket. Different ones would shake my hand and say, *"Praise the Lord, Brother Beuttler,"* and I would think, *"But where is my ticket?"*

The Manifest Presence of God

The Lord bore witness that this was the time to go, but still there was no ticket. Finally, an individual asked me, "*How are you going?*" and I replied, "*By boat.*" He said I would hardly get there, and it would be time to return. I explained that air travel was too expensive. In response, I was told that the difference would be given to me.

About halfway across the Atlantic, the Lord spoke to me saying, "*I have sent you on a journey.*" I was so pleased to know I was in the will of God. Since I had not known where to go, I was going home to my family in Germany. My mother was unsaved and was sick, so I thought I could talk to her about salvation and pray for her, which I did.

My sister told her pastor I was visiting, and I was asked to speak. The Lord woke me up early in the morning and gave me the message. The pastor asked me to come back the following night and I agreed. Again, the Lord woke me up, and as I sat in His presence, He gave me the message.

This went on day by day for a week. Then on Sunday morning the pastor said, "*Before you speak, I want to say something.*" I thought I was in trouble, because I had spoken on the Holy Spirit. Instead, he told the congregation that for many months, he had been praying that the Lord would give them the deeper things of the Spirit. He began to cry, and said, "*Just think, God sent a man from America to answer my prayers.*"

The Lord was indeed confirming the call that He had given me, and this was the beginning of my ministry to the Nations.

Chapter 3

Divine Appointments

The trip to Germany where I ministered in my sister's Church was the beginning of a ministry that reached around the world. The pastor had said, *"Just think, God sent a man from America to answer my prayers."*

While this was taking place, the Lord had something further in mind. One morning, He spoke to me. These words stood within me exactly as I am saying here. *"About the middle of the afternoon on New Year's Day, go by air to Amsterdam."* I responded, *"Lord, New Year's Day is a holiday and I would like to spend it with my mother. I have been away for many years."*

Again the impression became strong. *"Go to Amsterdam by air on New Year's Day in the middle of the afternoon."* Again I said, *"Lord, I have never been in Amsterdam and I would like to spend New Year's Eve with my mother, as this is special in Germany."*

The Lord spoke the same a third time. Then I remembered the time I had been told by the Lord to get a passport. I said to myself, "*Beuttler, are you going to miss God again?*" Then I said, "*yes*" to the Lord.

I went to the airport at Stuttgart and asked about a flight to Amsterdam on New Year›s Day. They told me there were no flights that day. I went to KLM and they told me it was a holiday and that absolutely nothing would be flying to Amsterdam on New Year's Day. Now I was in trouble, as I had taught much on "*divine guidance*," and I was stumped.

I went outside into a miserable mixture of rain, snow, and sleet, and stood on the sidewalk. I shut my eyes and spoke to God, "*Father, do you know the airline schedules?*" There was no answer, and I was almost in panic. I thought how can I ever again teach people about "*knowing the will of God*," if I make a mistake like this?

Then a thought came, "*Go to the American Express Company and see what they say*." I will never forget the man at their counter. There was a huge book of airline schedules, and he went back and forth through it. He asked the second time where I was going. Again, he went back and forth in the book. Then he asked which afternoon I wanted to go. Again, he went back and forth in the book.

He said, "*You are fortunate. There is a special non-stop flight going from Stuttgart to Amsterdam on New Year's Day at 4:10 in the afternoon.*" The Spirit so strongly bore witness within me that I shouted, "*That is it!*" I purchased my ticket and on New Year's Day, I went to Amsterdam.

When I arrived, I had no idea as to what I was to do and stood there, feeling nothing. So I prayed, "*Father, this is the airport in Amsterdam and I am here. Unless you speak, I will go into the city, check into a hotel, and tomorrow morning at eight o'clock, I will go to London.*" I had an appointment in London on that day. I still heard nothing, so I went into the city and found a hotel room.

Before I went to bed, I said, "*Father, I am here in the hotel. I am going to bed now, and if you do not tell me what I am to do, then tomorrow morning at eight o'clock I will go to the airport and fly to London.*"

In the morning I was up early and prayed, "*Father, I am still in Amsterdam and I am getting ready to go to the airport.*" The Lord did not speak. So I went to the airport and bought a ticket for a British European Airlines flight to London.

I went to my seat on the plane, and at eight o'clock we were ready to depart. We sat there, and the plane did not move. About fifteen minutes later an announcement was made, "*Will all passengers please return to the terminal building as a heavy fog has settled over the airport and it is too dangerous to take off.*"

I went into the lounge and suddenly, an enveloping presence of God came upon me. Oh, what a presence this was. Within and without, I was in a cloud of God's presence. A spirit of worship and prayer came upon me, so I found a comfortable chair in a corner and sat there. There was such an intense presence that I sat in an attitude of worship and prayer and lost track of everything.

After some time, I thought I should check and see about

the flight to London. I was amazed that it was now one o'clock in the afternoon and that I had been sitting there all that time. I walked over to the window and the fog was still so heavy that only the barest outline of things could be seen. They had cancelled all flights and nothing was coming in or going out.

As I stood there, two men were in front of me. One worked at the airport and the other appeared to be a passenger. The airport worker said, "*We do not understand this fog. There is no fog anywhere, except at this airport.*" At first I thought nothing of it, but later the understanding came.

I stood there and figured how many dollars I was wasting per hour while sitting at this airport, doing nothing. Then the presence lifted and I felt empty, confused, and alone. I felt that I had somehow failed the Lord. I walked some and noticed a long table, like a dining room table. No one was there, so I went to one corner of it and sat down.

The following details are very important. I sat there wondering where I had made my mistake. Then I looked to my left and a man, immaculately dressed in a black suit, was walking toward me. He appeared to be an unusual man as he walked very erect, yet not stilted. His bearing was regal and he was an unusually good-looking man. I wondered who he could be. I thought he must be a member of a royal family.

Then he sat down just opposite where I sat. Paying no more attention to him, I closed my eyes and spoke to God, "*Father, where am I?*" I felt I had gone astray and wanted the Lord to let me know what had happened. For no reason that I can explain, I then looked at the man opposite me. At that very moment, he lifted a book from his attaché case. He opened it before me as though he would read it. I saw the title of the book, which said, "*I AM leading you where you do not wish to go.*" Then he closed the book and returned it to his attaché case, as though he had changed his mind. I had my answer from God.

A waiter came and asked us both if we would move, as they needed the table to feed some passengers. I went one way, and this "*man*" went out of the building into the fog, and disappeared. Since this incident, the Lord has twice born witness to me (*once publicly and once privately*) that he was the Angel of the Lord whom God had sent to the airport to bring me back into His will.

As I continued to walk and look for a seat, I apologized and asked the Lord to forgive me. Then His presence returned. All I wanted was to sit in His presence as I had before, but my chair was taken. I noticed a nice comfortable chair next to a round table. There was a black man sitting on one side, and the opposite chair was empty. I quickly sat down before someone else got it.

As I shut my eyes to let my spirit go up to commune with God, this man interrupted me. He said, "*Sir, tell me your secret.*" I opened my eyes and found him leaning across the table toward me. I said, "What secret?" He said, "*Sir, I have been watching you as you sat in that chair all morning. What was that light on your face?*"

I said, *"What light?"* He responded, *"You had a light on your face, and I wondered to myself if you had what I am seeking. Sir, if you have what I am seeking, will you please tell me your secret. I am a businessman from East Africa, and I was brought up in the Mohammedan faith. But, Mohammed has never given me peace. I need my sins forgiven and I do not know how. I desire true peace."*

He told me that he had tried many different religions, but had not found what he sought for. Then he said, *"I have given up all religions and every day for many years I have prayed one prayer. 'Oh God, if there is a God, show me the way to true peace.' Sir, do you know the way to true peace and if you do, will you please tell me your secret?"*

During this time, the Lord put within me what I should say. I shared with him the story of my conversion in New York, when I had looked for peace. Now, at this airport in Amsterdam, it was my privilege to lead this man to Jesus Christ, the Prince of Peace.

The fog had continued to be so thick that nothing moved. As I finished my testimony, and for the second time used the Scripture, *"Believe on the Lord Jesus Christ and you shall be saved,"* an announcement was made, *"We will depart in ten minutes. The fog has lifted."* I finished my testimony and we said good bye.

The Lord heard this man praying in East Africa and in His providence brought him to Amsterdam. He also brought me to Germany and gave me the time I should go to Amsterdam. When we were both there at the same time,

He used a fog to close the Airport so He could answer this man's prayer. And when I lost my way, He sent His angel to turn me back into His presence. Then, He brought us together in that busy airport. As soon as the testimony was given, God lifted the fog and the planes were flying again. He went his way, and I went to London.

This is a testimony of an *"outworking of the personal knowledge of God"* that I had received while praying in a motel room. Again, Satan had tried to destroy it, but it was saved through the intervention of the Angel of the Lord.

If we will allow ourselves to be led into this area of the *"knowledge of God"* and *"His manifest presence,"* we will have experiences, which will confirm the Scripture that Paul wrote to the Corinthians:

"...Eye has not seen, nor ear heard, neither have entered into the heart of man, the things which God has prepared for them that love Him."
I Corinthians 2:9

This is quoted from Isaiah, which reads:

"For since the beginning of the world men have not heard, nor perceived by the ear, neither hath the eye seen, O God, beside You, what He has prepared for him that waits for Him."
Isaiah 64:4

If we will give ourselves to God and His purposes, things we have never seen, heard of, or even imagined, will be waiting for us *"in His presence."*

Chapter 4

Face to Face

"And Moses said to the Lord... Now therefore, I pray You, if I have found grace in Your sight, Show me now Your way, that I may know You, that I may find grace in Your sight: and consider that this nation is Your people. And He said, My presence shall go with you, and I will give you rest."

"And he said to Him, If Your presence go not with me, carry us not up from here. For wherein shall it be known here that I and Your people have found grace in Your sight? is it not in that You go with us? so shall we be separated, I and Your people, from all the people that are upon the face of the earth."
Exodus 33:12-16

In this passage, Moses said, *"so shall we be separated."* The idea being that the *"distinguishing mark"* between the Lord's people and other nations was to be the *"presence of God."* So also today, the presence of God should distinguish His people from all others.

Moses knew this people and was reluctant to lead them into the promised land, as they were a stubborn and rebellious nation. Therefore he asked, "*Show me now Your way that I may know You.*" We can learn to know God through His ways, what He does and how He accomplishes it. Moses understood that, as we watch God at work, we learn something about His character and His nature.

The Lord's ways differ from ours. Some time ago, Hattie Hammond told me something that I will never forget. She had been in a large convention. A young man spoke and she said she had never heard anything worse than the way that young fellow harangued the people. Yet when he finished, the power of God fell and the people stood and worshipped as the Lord poured His Spirit out upon them. She was surprised and questioned the Lord, "*How can You bless a harangue like we just heard?*"

Then the Lord explained that He was not blessing one word of what the man had said, but He was pouring the "*Spirit of rejoicing*" upon His people to help them "*forget*" what had been said.

I thought, the next time I rejoice for the Lord's blessing after I speak, I will consider that maybe He is just using His eraser. A word such as this teaches us something about God.

There is such a thing as "*the personal knowledge of a personal God.*" We can come to know Him, and begin to understand His ways through the "*manifestation of His presence*" as He makes Himself known to us.

Moses asked that he might come to personally know the Lord. He was not speaking about an intellectual knowledge of God. We do need to know and be informed, but Moses sought to have a personal acquaintance with a personal God, through a personal experience.

My daughter has many books about Queen Elizabeth and sought to learn all she could about her. One year, I was able to take her with me to France. We stopped in London on our way to Paris. Because she was so fond of the Queen, I took her to Buckingham Palace to see the royal guard.

She said, *"Daddy, do you think we will see the Queen?"* She was very disappointed when I told her it was not possible. The Queen was there, but because of a lack of relationship, we were unable to personally meet her. Although my daughter could share all kinds of things about the Queen, she still did not know her.

But the Lord is available to all those who seek to personally know Him, as He desires us to *"experientially"* know Him.

"And the Lord spoke to Moses face to face, as a man speaks to his friend...."
Exodus 33:11

Moses had a personal relationship with the Lord, and the Lord was available to him. Here is a man so intimate with God that we are told that God spoke with him *"face to face."* This means directly, not in some indirect way through a vision, dream, or a prophet. Although Moses knew the Lord personally, he still prayed, *"show me now Your way, that I may know You."* In other words, Moses desired to know the Lord even better.

In a morning Chapel service, I spoke to the students about seeking God. Afterwards, I was challenged by someone who said, *"Why do you exhort these students to seek God when they have already found Him?"* This person did not understand the personal knowledge of God. My answer to him was that the students *"need"* to know the Lord even *"more."* There is no limit to the disclosure of God to our hearts.

There were three areas in which Moses had a special knowledge of the Lord. First, he had an intimate relationship with the Lord.

> **"And there arose not a prophet since in Israel like to Moses, whom the Lord knew face to face."**
> ***Deuteronomy 34:10***

Second, he experienced intimate communion with the Lord.

> **"And the Lord spoke to Moses face to face, as a man speaks to his friend...."**
> **Exodus 33:11**

Third, he had an intimate privilege.

> **"With him will I speak mouth to mouth, even apparently, and not in dark speeches; and the similitude of the Lord shall he behold: wherefore then were you not afraid to speak against My servant Moses?"**
> **Numbers 12:8**

Notice that the Lord is very concerned about how we talk about those who are His personal friends.

Concerning this privilege, the Lord said, *"and the similitude of the Lord shall he behold."* In my study, I use different translations to gain understanding, as they throw different rays of light on a particular subject.

The jewels of the kings and queens of England are kept in the tower of London. Among them is a huge diamond that I have carefully looked at. From one view, it appears to have a yellow sparkle. From a different angle, it is green. From another, it is red or blue. There are different colors, but it is the same diamond. These translations are to me as this diamond.

In the King James Version the term, *"the similitude of the Lord"* is used. In another version, *"the form of the Lord shall he behold."* A different translation reads, *"the shape of the Lord shall he behold."* Even though God is a Spirit and does not have a material body, He has a localized appearance. The Lord gave Moses the privilege to behold this similitude, likeness, shape, and form of God.

Jesus prayed, *"And this is life eternal, that they might know You the only true God, and Jesus Christ, whom You have sent"* (John 17:3). He desired His disciples to know God.

> **"For I desired mercy, and not sacrifice; and the knowledge of God more than burnt offerings."**
> **Hosea 6:6**

In the days of Israel, the Lord was more interested in their "*knowing*" Him than in all their "*sacrifices*" and "*gifts.*" In Jeremiah 24:7, we have a pertinent statement: "*And I will give them a heart to know Me.*"

In the final analysis, the true knowledge of God is a "*matter of the heart.*" This involves an inner "*capacity*" and "*capability*" to enter into a personal relationship with God.

This is my prayer for all of us,

"*Lord, give us a heart, the capacity and the capability, to know You in personal experience.*"

Chapter 5

Glory about Him

"But let him that glories glory in this, that he understands and knows Me, that I am the Lord which exercise loving kindness, judgment, and righteousness in the earth; for in these I delight, says the Lord."
Jeremiah 9:24

The Lord *"delights"* in those who know and understand Him. This speaks of a humble, grateful appreciation. I can relate to this through an experience with my daughter.

I had just returned from a ministry trip to South America, and I usually brought a special present for my daughter. Because I had not done so this time, I said to her, *"I am so sorry that I do not have something special for you."* She responded, *"Daddy, that's all right, you are my best present and the nicest daddy I ever had."* This, all the more caused me to want to buy something very special for her.

The Lord desires us to *"glory about Him"* in simplicity and in gratefulness. He evidently agrees with the statement, *"Joys not shared are only half enjoyed."* The Lord loves to enter into our joys, and when we glory about Him, His heart is touched, as He has feelings too.

God has an emotional nature, and He expresses emotions. He has a social nature, and He enjoys our fellowship and rejoices with us, for His Word tells us, *"In these things I delight, says the Lord."*

Some years ago, I attended a Bible Study. At the end, the pastor asked me to close in prayer. I was so filled with the *"Spirit of rejoicing"* that I was unable to pray or dismiss the meeting. All I could do was shout, *"Hallelujah."* The Spirit of this worship spread over the people and almost everyone began to praise the Lord.

When it again became quiet, there was a prophetic message, which said, *"God is pouring out His Spirit of rejoicing upon His people because one who had been a sinner has repented, and there is so much joy in heaven that the Lord is sharing this with His people so that He and they may rejoice together."*

When I was a student in Bible School, I was talking to the Superintendent of the Denomination to which I belonged. Later, his son came into the room and asked, *"What will you do when you leave?"* I had no home, as my family lived in Germany, and could only reply, *"I do not know."* Then he asked what ministry I thought I would have. Again, I could only say, *"I do not know."*

The Manifest Presence of God

Then he said, "*I am glad I am not like you. I know people at the top, and I will have a big church.*" When he left the room, he slammed the door and it felt like a shot from a gun going through my heart. It really hurt because I had nowhere to go. I dropped to my knees and prayed a very simple prayer, "*Father, did You hear what he said?*"

As I prayed this, in a flash of revelation, the Lord quickened these thoughts to me. "*It is true that he knows people at the top. But it is also true that I am your Father, and that I am at the top of all those who are at the top. And, I am your personal superintendent.*" I lifted my hands and said, "*Father, thank You for being Who You are. This day I acknowledge You as my personal superintendent.*" Years later, while in Rio De Janeiro, I was told that this fellow was working as a butcher, and he did not have the big church he thought he would have.

God responds to simple sincerity. In New Guinea, they know how to touch the heart of the Lord. In very poor English, they pray, "*Oh, Papa God, You nice fellow upstairs. Me no any good but You nice Papa God.*" The Lord responded to the sincerity of their heart and the simplicity of their prayer.

For example, when I was a youngster in Germany, I had always desired to see the Azores Islands. I do not know why, but they had captured my boyhood imagination. Many years later, I had made many trips to Europe, but never by way of the Azores, as only first class passengers were routed this way. I was to go to Rome, so I laid my itinerary before the Lord. I felt His witness that I was to go, so I arranged my ticket.

A short time before I left, I noticed in the newspaper that the airlines were routing Tourist Class travel to Europe by way of the Azores. I thought, how often I have wanted to stop at the Azores and now it is possible. Yet, I felt that I was in the will of God with the route I had already chosen. I prayed as I had before. I said, *"Father, did You by any chance read this newspaper article about the Azores?"*

Some would say this is foolish, as God knows everything and does not need to read the newspaper to find out. I know this very well. But I also know that the Lord hears and responds when I come to Him in this simple, practical way. This speaks of *"relationship,"* and of *"intimacy."*

I added to my prayer, *"Father, I have wanted to go that way for so long, and now I am going the other way. I just wonder what You think about this."* The Lord responded, not in words, but a witness as though He were saying, *"If you would like to change your route, I have no objections."* I just knew I had His permission and blessing to change, so I did.

When I returned to the school in the fall, I told the students about this, because I was really pleased. I thought God was so considerate in allowing me to change my route. It is amazing what God will do for us. When we respect His wishes, He will have regard for ours.

As soon as I had finished telling the students about this, a girl gave an utterance in tongues and one of the fellows interpreted it. The word said, *"God is pleased when He sees that He can please His children. For He loves to please His own and He rejoices in their pleasure."* When God saw that I was happy, then He was happy.

> **"But let him that glories glory in this, that he understands and knows Me... for in these things I delight, says the Lord."**
> **Jeremiah 9:24**

One time I was going to Africa, and I looked at the route I would be taking and noticed Thebes on the Nile River in Egypt. I thought it would be nice to see the ancient ruins of Thebes and the temple of Karnak with its famous columns. I knew that I had nothing to do there, but as I looked at my map, I received a witness. The Lord quickened to me that I could stop at Thebes.

It was such a thrill to see the fulfillment of prophecy there. The plain where this powerful, beautiful city once stood was now just a vast open area. After I returned home, one of the teachers said to me, *"What did you see?"* I said, *"There was nothing left on the west side of the Nile where the main part of the city stood."*

He then told me that he had wondered why I wanted to stop there, as he knew I would not see anything. I responded that I had seen much. I knew that this was where this great city was located, which was one of the seven wonders of the ancient world. God had said that He would remove it from the earth.

What I saw was the tremendous power of Almighty God, the veracity of His Word of Prophecy, that He could obliterate such a huge city. I saw the might of God in an empty place.

> **"At that time Jesus answered and said, I thank You, O Father, Lord of heaven and earth, because You have hidden these things from the wise and prudent, and have revealed them to babes. Even so, Father: for so it seemed good in Your sight."**
> **Matthew 11:25-26**

Notice, that the Lord deliberately withholds some truths from those who are *"wise and prudent."* This is not necessarily those who are educated, or knowledgeable. Rather, this refers to those who *"feel"* that they know it all. The problem with them is that they do not know enough to know that they do not know. Thus, they are *"unteachable."*

The Lord *"hides"* the precious, special things from these, such as the knowledge of His presence. The babes to whom He reveals these things are those who are simple, humble, lowly, and willing to learn. Their spirits are *"open"* to His manifest presence.

The Word tells us, *"No man can come to Me, except the Father which has sent Me draw him"* (John 6:44). Due to sin, there is no desire for God in the fallen human nature. Whenever a person has an interest in God, it is due to the *"activity"* of the Spirit of God.

If God gives us a hunger for Himself, this desire has been produced by the Spirit of God, because that for which we hunger is capable of being attained. The very hunger that we have for more of God is not only God›s call to get us to move in that direction, but it is also the guarantee that we can attain to that for which we hunger, if we will keep following in the direction of the hunger.

The attitude of heart that qualifies us is that we become as a "*babe.*" When a baby becomes hungry, it manifests that hunger by crying. The child cries and is fed by the mother. The baby does not ask for a chemical analysis of what it is being fed. There is something within that corresponds to the hunger, and the child just eats. But if an attempt is made to feed mustard to the baby, he will no longer eat. There is something there that does not appeal.

So it is spiritually. The Lord gives us a hunger and we may not know what we are hungry for, except that we have a sense of need and desire something from God. We may hear a message with truth that we have never heard. Though we do not understand it, within us, it is as with the baby. We eat and feel satisfied. We know this is a work of the Holy Spirit because we feel His witness and we feel good. We do not know how we know; we just know that we know.

So also, when an attempt is made to feed something to us that is not right, the witness is lacking and it does not set right within. We know that we should not partake.

Jesus said that except we become as children, we cannot enter the Kingdom. This is because we are moving beyond our capacity to understand. Thus the Lord releases the "*deeper things,*" only where there is this "*child-like*" faith.

It is only in this child-like faith that we are able to come to the Lord and express our love and appreciation for Him, even as my daughter expressed her appreciation for me, when I returned home without a present for her.

Chapter 6

God's Deep Secrets

**"Thus says the Lord, Let not the wise man glory in his wisdom, neither let the mighty man glory in his might, let not the rich man glory in his riches: But let him that glories glory in this, that he understands and knows Me, that I am the Lord which exercise loving kindness, judgment, and righteousness, in the earth: for in these things I delight, says the Lord."
Jeremiah 9:23-24**

God is infinite, but we are finite. Therefore, we cannot fully know or comprehend God. But in many of His ways, the Lord desires to be both known and understood.

**"The secret things belong to the Lord our God: but those things which are revealed belong to us and to our children for ever, that we may do all the words of this law."
Deuteronomy 29:29**

There are two areas of knowledge concerning God; the things which are "*secret*," which are known only to Him, and those things that are "*revealed*," which can be discovered only under certain conditions.

The Godhead is an example of the secret things, which belong to God. The Lord has never revealed how He can be three, yet only one at the same time. We may attempt illustrations, but none are satisfactory. Also, the fact that God has everlastingly existed without having a beginning is beyond our ability to comprehend.

The Lord placed Adam and Eve in the Garden of Eden and told them that they could freely eat the fruit of all the trees, except one particular tree. Man is spoken of as being a free-moral agent, able to do as he wills. However, the Word of God does not indicate the absolute freedom of man. Rather, man is limited, "*Of all these things you may freely eat, BUT.*"

In the original intention, the freedom of man as a free moral agent was circumscribed; he was not totally free, rather he was limited as he had been created to be dependent. "*You may go outside the circle of My will if you so choose, but if you do, such and such will take place.*" Therefore, man's freedom was relative rather than absolute.

Adam and Eve were under duress. If they went beyond the freedom given them, there was a resultant consequence. Also, the Lord has placed a limit on our knowledge of good. If we, with intellectual curiosity seek to go beyond the circle of divine revelation, and attempt to press into things, which God has not revealed, we will get into trouble.

For instance, our pursuing the origin of sin. We may trace it back to Satan and find that there was pride in his heart. But what originated this pride? God must have created the capacity, or given consent that pride could develop in Satan's heart.

If we press this kind of rationale, we will find, before we become aware of it, that a question is raised concerning the holiness and integrity of God. We have placed the Lord in the position of being a defendant, with our being the prosecutor. This will result in infidelity, and in time, our rejection of God. All this may happen because we are pressing beyond the limits of that which belongs unto us.

In their curiosity, some Bible teachers have attempted to press beyond the limits of divine restraint, and intrude into the things, which God has kept from man. For instance, how God deals with those who have never heard the Gospel. Many false and destructive doctrines have developed in this very way.

"And the Lord God commanded the man, saying, Of every tree of the garden you may freely eat. But of the tree of the knowledge of good and evil, you shall not eat of it: for in the day that you eat thereof you shall surely die."
Genesis 2:16-17

Some years ago, I visited a particular lady. I kept ringing the doorbell, as I knew she was always at home. Finally she answered and said, *"Please excuse me, as it took a long time for me to find the will of God as to whether I should open the door to you or not."*

She said, *"I believe in being spiritual, and I do nothing without first asking God. I ask Him about all my personal affairs, and even about what I should wear."* This goes beyond the intention of God, as He has given us latitude - "*of every tree ... you may freely eat, but...*"

We do not need to ask the Lord concerning which dress, suit, or shoes, we wear. There are many things in the area of our daily lives in which the Lord has given us the sense and wisdom to simply make our own choice, but there is a limit - "*But.*" Here, God established this limitation.

God can be adequately understood within the sphere of those things, which belong to us.

We must learn to respect the silence of God, and when God does not wish to explain, we should be content. God shares some of His secrets with some of His people, but not everything with everyone.

We tell certain secrets to our friends, but the older we become, the less we tell, because we have learned. God is very judicious, but He does share secrets with some.

> **"And the Lord said, shall I hide from Abraham that thing which I do."**
> **Genesis 18:17**

The Lord shared with Abraham the fact that He was about to destroy Sodom and Gomorrah.

> **"The secret of the Lord is with them that fear Him; and He will show them His covenant."**
> **Psalm 25:14**

One year, I was speaking to a group of ministers in an old castle in the Pyrenees Mountain area of France and mentioned this verse. One minister said to me, *"Do you know that in the French bible, this reads, 'the intimate communion of the Lord is with them that fear Him."*

This fear speaks of a reverential respect. Thus, our attainment of an intimate knowledge of God involves our relationship to Him. In Matthew 11:25, the attitude, which will bring us into this intimate knowledge, is given.

> **"At that time Jesus answered and said, I thank You, O Father, Lord of heaven and earth, because You have hidden these things from the wise and prudent, and have revealed them to babes."**

We must set aside our intellect and submit to the activity of the Holy Spirit in order to receive the understanding of His ways.

> **"That the God of our Lord Jesus Christ, the Father of glory, may give to you the spirit of wisdom and revelation in the knowledge of Him. The eyes of your understanding being enlightened; that you may know what is the hope of His calling, and what the riches of the glory of His inheritance in the saints.**

**And what is the exceeding greatness of His power to us-ward who believe, according to the working of His mighty power."
Ephesians 1:17-19**

To receive the knowledge of God involves our having esteem for, and placing great value upon the knowledge of God. For instance, in Proverbs 2:4:

"If you seek her as silver, and search for her as for hidden treasures."

Most all of the choicest things of God lie beneath the surface, and they must be searched out. These are not for the lukewarm, or the half-hearted, but for those who are earnest and have a heart appreciation of these things, and who demonstrate this by going after them, with effort.

Some things are not obtainable without our contending to succeed, as in an obstacle course. For instance, Moses put the tent of the Tabernacle afar off.

**"And Moses took the tabernacle, and pitched it outside the camp, afar off from the camp, and called it the Tabernacle of the congregation. And it came to pass, that every one which sought the Lord went out to the Tabernacle of the congregation, which was outside the camp."
Exodus 33:7**

Moses did not make it easy or convenient, rather, he put it *"out-of-the-way"* so it would take an effort to enter. Those who truly sought the Lord gladly made the effort. This was in fact a way of separating the wheat from the chaff, the *"earnest"* from the *"indifferent."* The Lord has a way of separating people.

One time I attended a service where the pastor understood the *"ways of God."* When the altar service would begin, he would sit on the platform and do nothing for a considerable time, until many had left. Then he would begin to minister to those who were sincere in their seeking of the Lord, and, there were remarkable results.

Later, I asked him why he waited so long. He responded, *"I wait until I know that only those who are truly seeking the Lord are present."* He knew that the earnest would stay, and the half-hearted would leave after a short time.

The Lord not only has a way of testing our earnestness, but He assesses us from the effort that we are willing to make. Only then will He begin to share the secrets of His presence.

Chapter 7

The Knowledge of God

**"If you seek her as silver, and search for her as for hidden treasures; Then shall you understand the fear of the Lord, and find the knowledge of God."
Proverbs 2:4-5**

We are to place a very high premium on the true *"knowledge of God."*

Suppose a large sum of money was buried near us, which would be ours if found. We would not sit and think about it, but rather, we would begin to search for it.

The *"treasure"* of the knowledge of God that is *"hidden within"* the Word of God is of far greater value than any earthly fortune. And, it also requires that we search for it. This heavenly treasure is purposely hidden, because it is not intended for those who are half-hearted, or indifferent.

There are three tests concerning our qualification to

partake of the knowledge of God; it is to be *"highly valued, earnestly desired, and diligently sought after."*

Moses asked that he might understand the ways of God.

> **"...If I have found grace in Your sight, show me now Your way, that I may know You."**
> **Exodus 33:13**

The Lord responded to this desire:

> **"My presence shall go with you, and I will give you rest."**
> **Exodus 33:14**

The knowledge of God and His manifest presence are closely related.

One year, I had laid before the Lord my itinerary from Philadelphia to Los Angeles, Tokyo, Hong Kong, Manila, and Singapore. I did not know which way to go from there, as I had invitations which required completely different routes. I could go south to Australia and then back to the west coast, or westward through Europe to the east coast.

I said, *"Father, I do not know where to go after Singapore."* I then waited in His presence, and suddenly the Lord spoke. The words were, *"I will meet you at the pyramids."* I knew what He meant, and accordingly laid out the rest of my trip.

In due time, around 3:30 AM, we were approaching Cairo, on an Indian Airlines flight, and I wondered where the

The Manifest Presence of God

Lord would meet me. I said we, as I was alone, but not alone. There is a hotel near one of the pyramids where I stopped several times to rest. I had sat there alone for hours, looking out across the desert toward the pyramids. I thought that this was where the Lord would meet me.

As I watched the city lights in the distance, there suddenly came a strong manifest presence of the Lord. He had come to me before we arrived, and I entered into that lovely country, distinctly aware of His being with me. It was as the Lord had said to Moses, *"My presence shall go with you, and I will give you rest."*

To *"experience"* the *"manifest presence of the Lord"* is a marvelous reality, which quickens and renews every aspect of our being. It produces a *"deep inner satisfaction"* that cannot be explained, only experienced.

In John 4:24, Jesus said, *"God is a Spirit."* In Luke 24:39, He said, *"Behold My hands and My feet, that it is I Myself: handle Me, and see; for a spirit has not flesh and bones, as you see Me have."*

When Jesus was born of Mary, a change took place in the Godhead. The second person of the Godhead, Jesus, took on a body. From that time, one member of the triune Godhead, has a body.

The first person of the Godhead, the Father, is also a person. He can see, feel, hear, and speak. He has a will and emotions. God has all of the attributes of personality, yet He does not have a body. Paul said, *"Absent from the body, present with the Lord."* When we die we are no less a person after our death than we were before our death.

Paul called this body a house. Thus we are not seen, but rather, the house in which we live. Someday, we will vacate it, but still live. This is important, as we must differentiate between personality and corporeality, or a material body. Therefore, I think of God as being a person regardless of the fact that He does not have a material body.

Consider Numbers 12:8:

> **"With him will I speak mouth to mouth, even apparently, and not in dark speeches; and the similitude of the Lord shall he behold...."**

"*Similitude*" speaks of the form, shape, or likeness of the Lord. Thus, it can be said that even though God is a Spirit personality, He nevertheless has a form.

Some theologians say these terms are "*anthropomorphic.*" That is, the words that signify form are only used to convey the aspect of spirit being. But to apply this to the shape and form of God is to destroy much spiritual truth in the Word, which should be taken as literal.

For example, the revelation of the shape and form of God is explicit in the following passage of Scripture.

> **"And the Lord said, Behold, there is a place by Me, and you shall stand upon a rock: And it shall come to pass, while My glory passes by, that I will put you in a cleft of the rock, and will cover you with**

The Manifest Presence of God

**My hand while I pass by: And I will take away My hand, and you shall see My back parts: but My face shall not be seen."
Exodus 33:21-22**

The Word tells us, *"And there shall no man see Me and live."* This refers to the face of God, *"But My face shall not be seen."* When Jesus said, *"no man has seen God at any time,"* He is saying that no man has seen the face, or the full glory of God. But Moses saw other parts of God.

The Lord shielded Moses from seeing His face because, if in his curiosity, he turned to see the face of God, he would die, as he could not stand the revelation of the full glory of God. Notice that God speaks of His hands, His face, and His back. The implication is that God appeared to Moses in human form.

Although God is a Spirit personality with a non-material form, this Spirit form is similar to the human form. When God said let us make man after our own likeness and in our own image, He created man with a physical form like unto His general spiritual form.

**"And God said, Let Us make man in Our image, after Our likeness...."
Genesis 1:26**

**"And Adam lived a hundred and thirty years, and fathered a son in his own likeness, after His image; and called his name Seth."
Genesis 5:3**

Notice that the same terms are used concerning the form of God and of man. Therefore, it is logical to assume that there is a certain resemblance, as to form, between God and man.

The Word tells us that the "*pure in heart*" shall see God. As we come to the Lord in simple faith and trust, and wait upon Him, He will not only "reveal" His manifest presence to us, but He will make Himself "*known*" to us, in terms and ways we can understand.

Chapter 8

The Manifest Presence of God

"Can any hide himself in secret places that I shall not see him? says the Lord. Do not I fill heaven and earth? says the Lord."
Jeremiah 23:24

The Lord "*fills*" both heaven and earth. This is His "*omnipresence*," which is the fact of His being present, everywhere. This aspect of His presence may, or may not be revealed or felt. When it is revealed, it is simply a feeling of "*presence*," apart from the revelation of a person. The manifest presence of God is more than this. It speaks of a presence in which the Lord reveals Himself as a person with personality and feelings.

"He that has My commandments, and keeps them, he it is that loves Me: and he that loves Me shall be loved of My Father, and I will love him, and will manifest Myself to him."
John 14:21

This is more than spiritual, or inner perception. It means that the Lord will make Himself known to us through one or more of our five physical senses.

Several years ago, the Lord had been awakening me during the night. Usually, at precisely 2:30, I would become aware of His being present. This meant that I was to get up and sit in His presence; a half hour, an hour, or sometimes through the rest of the night.

The next night, I would experience the same thing. This was a strong presence, in which worship would rise up from deep within me. One time, the Lord came and stood at the foot of my bed. Then He audibly sang a song that had a special meaning for me.

The Lord would come into my room in many different ways. Often, He would wake me up by knocking. When I heard this knock, I noticed that it would be exactly 2:30. Usually, I could tell the intention of the Lord by the way He knocked. If it was something urgent, the knock would have that characteristic. Sometimes it would be hardly audible and so delicate that I knew He had come as a lover for a time of fellowship.

I began to wonder why the Lord almost always came at 2:30. I knew that scripturally, no hour is more significant than another. I sought the Lord concerning this, and He gave me the understanding that I desired.

Long before, I had learned that there was a higher purpose for the night times than just sleeping. The Lord has revealed many choice truths to me during the long nights, as I spent time in His presence by *"waiting upon Him."*

Then the Lord spoke this to me. *"By 2:30, you have had enough sleep so you will be able to commune with Me for a time without falling asleep. And when we finish, there is enough time left for you to receive adequate rest for your day's work."* Our Lord is very considerate and understanding. This caused me to love and respect Him even more.

This experience of an active relationship with the Lord in *"waiting upon Him"* requires more self-discipline than any other area of experience. I cannot stay up to watch the late show, or for any other distraction. Nor can I afford to socialize at night. When my time for bed comes, which is quite early, I excuse myself from whoever may be present, and go to bed.

My appointment with the Lord is of far greater importance.

One night, I was awakened as the Lord walked away from the foot of my bed. I saw Him for only a moment. He was dressed in white glistening garments and I heard the rustling of these garments. The closest I can come to this sound, by way of description, is to say that it was like the leaves on a poplar tree. These make a rustling sound when the wind blows. At the same time, my room became filled with the presence of the Lord.

I looked at my watch and it was exactly 2:30. I had placed a chair next to the stove, where I could be comfortable. I sat there in His presence, until a quarter to five. Then I said, *"Lord, do You mind if I go back to bed?"* I waited, and as there was no answer, I returned to my bed. After I fell asleep, two hands came over my shoulders and literally pulled me upright into a sitting position. I do not know how this could have happened, as I was in the room alone. I only know that it did, and that there is no possible human explanation for this experience.

Again, there was a strong manifestation of His presence. When this happened, it was five o›clock. I had been in bed for fifteen minutes. I stayed up in His presence until about seven o›clock. Then I said, *"Lord, I must get ready for school,"* and did so. At this time, I had no indication of what the purpose of the Lord might have been.

That morning, the subject in my first class was the book of Hosea. This is a wonderful book, in which God gives us an insight into His broken heart. I had been teaching only about ten minutes, when I sensed an unusual presence. I pushed back my book and said, *"Students, there is quite a presence here, let us pause and see what this means."*

At once, there came a powerful prophetic utterance and the classroom was electrified. Hands went up, and worship began to flow out from the students. Oh, such a presence of God.

Then everything became quiet and a girl began to beautifully sing. Her voice went to unusual highs, and then deep lows. It was as if she were in an opera. Another girl followed, and then sometimes they sang together in profound harmony, or answered each other in the spirit. After this, we were given the interpretation. It was the expression of a love relationship between the Lord and His Church. Then the power fell again, and there was profound rejoicing.

The class time passed and the bell rang. It was time to leave the classroom, but no one left. Everyone was taken up in praising the Lord. Another class came, but could not enter as we were still there. As they stood outside in the vestibule, wondering what they should do, the Holy Spirit fell on them, and they entered into the worship. Another hour went by, and all of us were still there.

Again the bells rang, and the third class came. We were still in the classroom; the vestibule was still filled with the second class, so the third class stood outside the building, wondering what they should do. Suddenly, the Holy Spirit fell on them, and they began to worship in a beautiful harmony with the others.

By noontime, the Holy Spirit had fallen upon the entire school. When dinnertime came, only a few out of several hundred were in the dining room. When Bible School students do not show up for dinner, there is one of three reasons. Either they are sick, in love, or there is revival. This was the beginning of a revival that lasted for ten days, in which God moved in a mighty way.

It had begun the night before, when I was literally pulled upright in my bed. I clearly believe that had I not rightly responded to this experience during the night, this revival would have been missed. It had its origin in my *"waiting upon the Lord"* during the hours of that night.

Walter Beuttler

Our responding to the presence of the Lord, and waiting upon Him "*in His presence*," is of tremendous value.

Chapter 9

Spiritual Sensitivity

Often, during the night season, the Lord comes and instructs me about *"spiritual sensitivity"* and *"responsiveness"* to His presence. During one of these times, the Lord strongly impressed me with this Scripture,

"...Do not I fill heaven and earth?"
Jeremiah 23:24

This has become such a reality to me that I have no problem in drawing nigh to the Lord, anywhere - at any time. No matter what environment I may be in, I know that the Lord is there with me.

I received a very practical lesson concerning this while on a trans-Atlantic flight. Suddenly, the plane turned and headed back. I looked out the window and saw what appeared to be a cloud coming from a wing. Then I saw the same thing happening in the other wing, so I thought the plane was on fire. Instead, gas was being dumped.

Then came the announcement, *"We are having a slight*

difficulty and are returning to the airport. We will prepare you for an emergency landing on the water, should it be necessary. Please take off your shoes, remove all objects from your pockets and tighten your belt as firmly as possible. Be prepared to place a pillow over your face."

They said we would gently land on the waves and wait for help to arrive. They made it sound easy, but I knew it was very dangerous. I then said goodbye to each of my family and committed myself to the Lord. This was the fourth time I have done this.

I prayed, *"Father, to the best of my knowledge, I am in Your will, and if this is the end, so be it; but Your Word says, Do not I fill heaven and earth? Father, if You fill heaven and earth, then You fill this airplane, therefore You and I are in this together, so if we go down, You also are going down."* As I said this, I felt an intense sense of His presence.

We did not need to land on the water, but made it safely to an airport. In those situations it is important to know that He does fill heaven and earth, and to understand what that means to us.

On another flight, I was over the Amazon Jungles in a plane that was having trouble. I sat by the window and watched as we came very close to the trees. The crew was serving sandwiches to keep the passengers occupied, but no one was eating them as they were watching the trees. Again, I had a profound sense that the Lord was in the plane with me and that He would bring us through safely.

Once again, on a flight in the same area, the lightning

was extremely severe, brilliantly lighting the sky with one flash after another. I sat there and wondered where it would hit next. It was so comforting to be able to say, *"Father, you and I are in this plane together."* To me, His omnipresence has become very personal and real. It is not merely a theological fact, but rather, an intense reality.

Jesus said in Matthew 6:6: *"Your Father which sees in secret shall reward you openly."* The word *"secret"* tells us that although we may be totally unaware of His presence, He is there, watching and listening. This knowledge of the omnipresence of God is a tremendous help in prayer. We may pray, feeling no response or presence - absolutely nothing; but in confidence we can say, *"Father, I know that You are here, and I thank You for Your presence."*

Whatever we may be doing, or wherever we may be, we can abide and rest in His presence, knowing that He is with us. And often, when we acknowledge His presence, though we may feel nothing, He will come and confirm the fact that He is present.

This manifestation of His omnipresence, which I experienced, can be spoken of as the localized, personalized, manifest presence of the Lord Jesus Christ. Jesus said: *"Except you eat the flesh of the Son of man, you have no life in you."* He was the visible embodiment of the truth of God.

If you will accept and eat these experiences that I share with you, the truth in these will also become meat in your spiritual life and experience. The Lord often uses my experiences as His way to impart His truth and life into others, who are spiritually hungry and desire to know Him.

These experiences are not just interesting stories, but the embodiment of the truth. They serve as illustrations, but they also are demonstrations of the truth so we may know how truth can be applied to our personal life experience. Also, it is important to know that there is a price which must be paid by those who would press onward into all that the Lord has to offer.

I had spent a weekend ministering in Altoona, Pennsylvania. Monday morning, I was at the railroad station reading the morning newspaper. I received a slight "*check*" in my spirit, and knew what it meant. This was a quickening of the Holy Spirit to call my attention away from what I was doing, to the Lord. I folded up the newspaper and said, "*Father, what do You want?*" At once I received a spirit of prayer and intercession, which lasted all the way to Philadelphia.

Each Monday night, I teach a class in Philadelphia, in connection with the Bible School where I am a teacher. When I arrived, I thought I would get a Chinese dinner, but again the Lord checked me. I knew that this meant that I was to continue praying. I returned to my room at the YMCA, and prayed until the time of the meeting.

When the time to teach came, I said, '*The Lord is present tonight*" and the power fell. At the end of that meeting, someone remarked, "*When you came in, we could feel the presence of God walk in with you."* I had spent all day in intercession, giving myself to the Lord. We had a marvelous move of the Holy Spirit for five consecutive Monday nights.

A pastor who did not like what was taking place, complained to the denomination to which I belong. Two officials came to my office at the Bible School. They said I was not doing any teaching in the night school, but was stirring up the people and that this was to stop. My response was that the Lord was pouring out His Spirit, and that needs were being met in profound ways. I added that I thought this visitation was a wonderful thing.

Then they said, *"We are receiving complaints and we want you to stop it."* I said, *"But what if the Holy Spirit continues? I did not start this visitation, I merely cooperated with the Spirit and put no hindrance in His way."* They responded, *"We believe that He is finished working."*

I asked, *"But, how do you know; you were not there."* Again they said, *"We want you to tell the students that the Spirit is finished working, and that you are going on with the classes."* Then they left.

A short time later, I was the speaker at a camp meeting, and the Holy Spirit wonderfully moved. Again the Church authorities came and said, *"We want you to stop whatever it is that gets you involved in these so-called movings of the Spirit. We are being told that whenever there is one of these stirrings, you are in the middle of it."* I had thought they would be glad that I had given myself to fasting and prayer, in obedience to the Holy Spirit.

That night I was unable to sleep for I felt very discouraged. My superiors were telling me to stop the moving of the Holy Spirit in the classes, and I was being criticized for having a move of the Holy Spirit in the camp meeting. I thought, "*I will quit.*"

The next night, I quickly fell asleep. At that time, we lived in a cottage, which had three wooden steps leading to the front door. I was awakened out of a deep sleep by heavy footsteps walking up these three steps. Somehow, I instinctively knew that this was the Lord. I heard Him take hold of the knob of the door. This knob usually rattled, and I heard it rattle. I heard Him turn the knob and pull the door open, step through the door, take hold of the inside knob and close the door.

I heard Him walk through the dinette. He stopped at the door to my bedroom and then He spoke in a rich, deep, masculine voice. He had come to reassure me that He was with me and that He would protect me against all my enemies. I clearly heard this audible voice with my physical ear.

After that, He turned and walked through the dinette, turned the knob and opened the front door and then closed it after He left. I heard Him go down the three steps. This was a personal visit from a personal Christ, in a time of deep distress, when I was about to turn my back on the movings of the Holy Spirit. This visit gave me the strength and will to continue, and to pay the price for His presence.

Later, I met with the pastor who I felt had complained and he acknowledged that he had done so. I asked if he would be interested in hearing how this move of the Holy Spirit had come about, and he said he would. After I shared with him, he bowed his head and tears literally flowed down his face and he asked if I would pray for him, that he might have such movings in his ministry. The Lord had visited, and then vindicated me.

I then asked the Lord if there was a Scripture which would confirm that I had literally heard the Lord walking. In response, the Lord drew my attention to Genesis 3:8.

"And they (*Adam and Eve***) heard the voice of the Lord God walking in the garden in the cool of the day."**

This word "*voice*" literally means "*sound*" and is translated this way in the Hebrew Bible. Adam and Eve had experienced the personalized presence of the Lord. I asked the Lord if there was another Scripture, and I was directed to I Samuel 3:10.

"And the Lord came, and stood, and called as at other times, Samuel, Samuel. Then Samuel answered, Speak; for Your servant hears."

The fact of this personal visitation from the Lord is established in John 14:21.

"He that has My commandments, and keeps them, he it is that loves Me: and he that loves Me shall be loved of My Father, and I will love him, and will manifest Myself to him."

The Lord loves everyone, but this love is for those who "*meet the conditions*" He sets forth. The evidence, or reciprocation of this love is that He will manifest Himself to them. In the original, this word "*manifest*" means that the Lord will make Himself "*personally real.*" Thus, Jesus is saying, "*I will plainly show Myself to him.*"

The Pulpit Commentary, which refers to Thayer's Greek Lexicon, says that this word "*manifest*" is so strong that it can mean nothing less than a manifestation of the presence of God, perceivable by one of more of our human faculties.

Thus, it is possible for each one of us to "*experience*" the personal presence of the Lord Jesus Christ in our lives.

Chapter 10

Manifestations of His Divine Presence

Those who "*set apart*" quality time to seek the Lord and in anticipation, "*wait*" in His presence, will be given "*revelations*" and "*openings*" in the Word and also, may be blessed with "*movings*" and "*manifestations*" of the Holy Spirit.

"The secret of the Lord is with them that fear Him; and He will show them His covenant."
Psalm 25:14

This "*fear*" is a worshipful reverence that moves the heart of the Lord to make known the "*treasures of darkness.*" These are spiritual nuggets and principles, which are buried beneath the "*letter of the Word*" and can be known only by "*revelation.*" To be valid, there must be a Scriptural basis for these experiences. We should not move into areas which go beyond the text and context of the Word of God.

"He that has My commandments, and keeps them, he it is that loves Me: and he that loves Me shall be loved

**of My Father, and I will love him, and will manifest Myself to him."
John 14:21**

For the Lord to *"manifest"* Himself to us means that He will make His presence *"known"* to us, through one or more of our physical senses. The following is a Scriptural example of this.

**"For the Lord had made the host of the Syrians to hear a noise of chariots, and a noise of horses, even the noise of a great host; and they said one to another, Lo, the king of Israel has hired against us the kings of the Hittites, and the kings of the Egyptians, to come upon us."
II Kings 7:6**

There were no horses or chariots, but the Syrians heard sounds as if they were there. Through this seeming *"sound,"* the Lord gave the Syrians the message He intended them to have.

I have often heard a sound that awakened me, as if the Lord had audibly knocked on a door that was close to my ear. The Lord was "causing" me to *"hear"* the sound of a knocking, which conveyed the message that it was time to get up and wait on Him. The fact that this knocking can be spiritual, rather than literal, is confirmed in the Song of Solomon.

"I sleep, but my heart wakes: it is the voice of my Beloved that knocks, saying, Open to Me, My sister, My love, My dove, My undefiled...." Song of Solomon 5:2

In Acts 2:2, another reference is made to sound. *"And suddenly there came a sound from heaven as of a rushing mighty wind, and it filled all the house where they were sitting."*

Here, the presence of the Holy Spirit was made known to those who were gathered in the Upper Room, through the *"sound"* of a rushing mighty wind. This indicated the initial coming of the Holy Spirit to abide within the believer, which had been promised by Jesus, and for which they were waiting.

This was the Lord, *"manifesting"* His presence through the medium of *"sound."* They heard with their physical ears the Holy Spirit come into their midst. This experience introduced them to the *"personal presence"* of the Holy Spirit.

Hattie Hammond told me that she heard, with her natural faculty of hearing, an entire (*spiritual*) orchestra playing during a visitation. Thus, on occasion, God may manifest His presence to us through a particular sound, which is perceivable to our human faculty of hearing, in order to convey a message to us.

This experience of our hearing an *"indication"* of the presence, or of the purpose of the Lord, should be a part of our spiritual experience. It will happen, or take place when, within the judgment of God, the occasion requires such.

Another way in which the Lord may manifest His presence to us, is through the faculty of *"smell."*

One time during a move of the Spirit, a fragrance wafted through the Chapel. It was recognized as the "*fragrance of the presence*" of the Lord. The wife of the music director attended this service while he stayed home with the children. When she returned home, he asked her about the perfume she was wearing. He was smelling the fragrance of the Lord from the meeting, which still clung to her clothing.

We should be responsive to, but never strain after manifestations, as they are altogether a matter of "*Divine discretion*." The Lord should never be told "*how*" He should meet us; for the prerogative of how belongs to Him. Rather, we should "*wait*" in His presence, "*open our spirits*" before Him, and then "*respond*" to whatever way He may move upon us in order to make His presence known.

I believe the Lord has given these manifestations to me that I might, as I minister throughout the world, let others know that these personal visitations from the Lord may occur, and then help them with their response to them.

I have been told by many that by sharing these experiences, I have helped them to understand various movings of the Holy Spirit which they had experienced. Once, after ministering from Revelation, "*Behold, I stand at the door and knock*," a lady said, "*I have been awakened many times by a sound of knocking, and once I heard my name being spoken. I thought there was something wrong with me. Now I understand that this was the Lord, and that I am to respond.*"

> **"And there appeared to them cloven tongues
> of fire, and it sat upon each of them"
> Acts 2:3**

The Word tells us that these manifestations *"appeared."* Those present actually saw something that looked like flames of fire. Here, the Lord was manifesting His presence through the medium of *"sight."*

> **"Now Moses kept the flock of Jethro his father in law, the priest of Midian... and the angel of the Lord appeared to him in a flame of fire out of the midst of a bush: and he looked, and, behold, the bush burned with fire, and the bush was not consumed. And Moses said, I will now turn aside, and see this great sight, why the bush is not burned. And when the Lord saw that he turned aside to see, God called to him out of the midst of the bush, and said, Moses, Moses. And he said, Here am I."
> Exodus 3:1-4**

This bush only looked as if it were burning, as it was not consumed. This manifestation of the presence of the Lord was used to arrest the attention of Moses. The Lord was patiently waiting for him to notice and respond. When he did, the Lord spoke to Him.

The Lord may use a special means to attract our attention, and will speak to us only after we respond. This flame, which seemingly burned, was a divine presence that is called the "Angel of the Lord." The practical lesson here is the fact that there is such a thing as a manifestation of the

Lord, which is perceivable to our human faculty of sight.

Israel had seen the presence of the Lord for forty years. By day they saw the Shekinah Glory of the Lord as a cloud, and by night, as the appearance of a fire. They were to follow this manifestation of the presence of the Lord, by moving when it moved, and staying when it stayed.

They were given these manifestations of the divine presence that they might learn the principles of guidance, as they were led through the wilderness.

"Now when all the people were baptized, it came to pass, that Jesus also being baptized, and praying, the heaven was opened, and the Holy Ghost descended in a bodily shape like a dove upon Him, and a voice came from heaven, which said, You are My beloved Son; in You I am well pleased." Luke 3:21-22

Here, the Holy Spirit descended upon Jesus in a bodily shape, like a dove. The Holy Spirit is a person with all the faculties of personality. He does not have a body, but He descended in a form that was like unto a body. He can take other forms to reveal His presence, as in the upper room; He used cloven tongues of fire to make Himself known. Thus, Spirit has form.

The Lord uses these varied manifestations as a means to make Himself known to us. Experiences such as these should be the norm for us, and not the exception.

It is important for us to understand that we are to look past whatever means the Lord may use to make His presence known to us, and respond to Him, as the manifestation of His presence indicates.

Chapter 11

Quickening Presence

"And Moses took the tabernacle, and pitched it outside the camp, afar off from the camp, and called it the Tabernacle of the congregation... And it came to pass, as Moses entered into the tabernacle, the cloudy pillar descended, and stood at the door of the tabernacle, and the Lord talked with Moses... And the Lord spoke to Moses face to face, as a man speaks to his friend...."
Exodus 33:7a, 9, 11

Through *"omnipresence"* the Lord is everywhere at one and the same time, which omnipresence fills both heaven and earth. This relates to His *"state of being"* and *"sovereign power."* Within His omnipresence, the Lord reveals Himself as being a person who makes Himself locally known through His *"manifest presence."*

There are two aspects to His manifest presence. The first is the Lord appearing to us as a *"person"* in which He makes known to us, through one or more of our five physical senses, a measure of His thoughts or feelings.

The second is the feeling of His presence as an *"inner glow"* which comes deep within us. This is a *"quickening presence"* which causes us to become keenly aware of the spiritual realm.

> **"My presence shall go with you,
> and I will give you rest."**
>
> **Exodus 33:14**

I usually travel alone, but not alone, because of the companionship of the presence of God. Last summer, I had meetings in Bangkok and changed planes in Singapore. We arrived at the Singapore airport early and a man said he would make sure my luggage was put on the right plane so I could be free to get something to eat.

When we arrived in Bangkok, several other large jets arrived around the same time. Passengers and luggage were everywhere, since the airport was small. All the other passengers from my plane had picked up their luggage, but my suitcases were not there. I went to the Tai-Airways desk and told them that apparently my luggage had been lost.

I decided to go to the hotel and wait for them to call when my luggage was found. Then I felt to go back to the conveyor one more time to see if it might have come while I was at the desk. I looked, but found nothing. Almost an hour and a half had passed and everyone was gone. I thought I must reconcile myself to the fact that my luggage was lost and buy replacements.

The Manifest Presence of God

Just as I was about to turn away, I felt the Lord›s quickening presence. It was so strong that it seemed as if the Lord was standing to my left, by the conveyor belt. I had an inner sense of calm as I felt the Lord had come to stand with me.

We stood there together, at the conveyor belt. I thought, if the Lord has come to stand here with me, I should not leave, so I kept looking at the conveyor belt. This lasted about fifteen minutes as I stood there, thanking the Lord for His presence.

Just then, my luggage appeared on the belt. It had been mixed with the luggage of another flight. I was so delighted because the Lord had come and stood with me so I would not leave. After I picked up my suitcases, I discovered that the Lord was no longer there. He came to help me because He knew my things would come. *"My presence shall go with you, and I will give you re*st."

"Oh how great is Your goodness, which You have laid up for them that fear You; which You have wrought for them that trust in You before the sons of men! You shall hide them in the secret of Your presence from the pride of man: You will keep them secretly in a pavilion from the strife of tongues."
Psalm 31:19-20

Here, the presence of the Lord is seen as being a shelter in which we are protected and vindicated, concerning that which others may say or do.

A teacher in the school where I taught was very critical of my overseas travels. She heard that I was planning to go to Liberia and asked when I planned to go. When I told her the first week of June, she responded that this was not the time to go, and said I should have heard from the Lord.

When I told her that I had heard from the Lord, she declared that I had not heard, and that I should have had better discernment. She told me that this was the worst time to go to Liberia as it rains so much that no one would be able to come to the meetings.

When I arrived in Liberia, there was sunshine each day and a full moon each night. They told me that they had never seen such beautiful weather during this season. When I returned home, I was able to tell her that we had a rainless week and that the presence of the Lord had been with me in an unusual way. As a result, her criticism was silenced. When the Lord speaks to us in His "*quickening presence*," we can depend on what He tells us.

One time, the Lord told me to go to France. However, I did not want to go because the Germans and French were traditional enemies and my father had fought against France. I said, "*Lord, I do not have money to go to France.*"

One evening during the summer camp meeting, the speaker said the Lord had told him to take up an offering for my travels. The amount of this offering was $580. The price of a return ticket to France was $552. Then I told the Lord my second excuse, "*Even though I have the fare, I still cannot go, as I have no contact.*" A few days later, a pastor asked me to minister in his Church and told me that he would like me to meet his friend from France, who was visiting.

After I spoke, this man said, *"Have you ever thought of coming to France?"* Just then, a strong presence of the Lord came, and I knew that I was to go, and made the arrangements to do so. When I arrived, I did not feel welcomed, as I was German. In fact, I overheard someone talking about me. Then I said, *"Father, do you hear what they are saying about me?"* When I said this, I felt a strong enveloping presence. It was the *"shelter"* of the presence of God. They still talked, and I still heard what they said, but now I had a fortress.

After the second morning meeting, I had come to know that they were not receptive to my ministry, and did not want me there. I felt very uneasy and told them I would like to go out for a walk. I had the feeling that they were relieved. Although it was cold and raining, I went to a park and sat there shivering. I said, *"Father, please let me go home as they do not want me or the message you gave me."* There was such a presence, but I did not receive anything from the Lord. Then I went back to my cold hotel room.

Once in my room, I said, *"Father, unless you do something I will find my ministerial grave in France."* I thought of the tens of thousands of white crosses I had seen as I traveled through Normandy by train.

Early Sunday morning, the Lord woke me up and gave me a message that had to do with His personal visits to me. I said, *"Lord, they will never receive this."* After I spoke for about ten minutes, I stopped and asked my interpreter to tell the congregation that someone had an utterance from the Holy Spirit.

"*Oh,*" she said, "*we do not do this in France. This is not our custom.*" I responded, "*Please do it anyway.*" She said, "*It just is not done like that.*" I said, "*Sister, the Holy Spirit has an utterance somewhere in the audience.*" We stood there arguing while they wondered what it was all about.

Finally she said, pointing a finger at me, "*Brother says somebody has an utterance from the Spirit and should give it.*" A lady stood up and gave a beautiful utterance in tongues. A man stood up and gave the interpretation. In the interpretation, God confirmed that He had sent me to France, that He was giving them His word, that He was seeking to bring them into a new dimension of experience in God, and that they should receive the word.

With that, the Spirit of God fell, hands went up and this large crowd began to shout and praise the Lord. I heard a voice at the other end of the platform I thought I recognized. The pastor who had criticized and opposed me had his hands raised and was shouting praises in French as tears ran down his face.

He came over, threw his arms around me, asked for my forgiveness, and said "*God has sent you to France, tomorrow we have a special outing for all the Churches, please stay and speak.*" This man was the leader of all my future visits, and opened many areas of France for my ministry. One year, they sent me to Japan, over the North Pole from Paris, and paid all the expenses.

The Manifest Presence of God

It was the presence of the Lord that held me steady, a shelter to envelop me, protect me, and shield me from their words until God could break through and turn hostility into friendship to the glory of God. These experiences in His manifest presence are real, and have a purpose.

Chapter 12

"When He Calls I Will Answer"

> "Behold, I stand at the door, and knock: if any man hear My voice, and open the door, I will come in to him, and will sup with him, and he with Me. To him that overcomes will I grant to sit with Me in My Throne, even as I also overcame, and am set down with My Father in His Throne."
> Revelation 3:20-21

One day as I sat before the Lord, He drew my attention to the above passage of Scripture. As I held this before the Lord, I began to see something on a higher level than I had before realized.

The Lord made known to me the "*method*" of His approach, in order to lead us into a feast with Him. The key to this is the word, "*attention.*" If I came to your house, I would not casually open the door, walk in and say, "*Hi, where is the refrigerator?*" Rather, I would first knock on the door to get your attention. After you responded to my knock, all else would follow.

So also, in Revelation 3:20, the Lord knocks to attract our attention. This knock may come in a number of different ways. For example, while on a TransPacific flight, I was thinking about some problems I would face when I returned home, when suddenly I felt a tug at my spirit, as something seeking attention.

Through past experiences, I recognized this as being the presence of the Lord, seeking to come and commune with me. I immediately stopped what I was doing, and turned aside into His presence, where we communed together. I can testify that these times of fellowship with the Lord have been profoundly satisfying and wonderful.

One time when I was in Australia, the pastor asked if I would return during the Christmas season for their ministers' seminar. He said that he also invited another minister and would arrange the tickets. I then told him I would come if he would promise not to place us on the same flight. If the Lord requested my attention while this minister was sitting next to me, I would need to become totally unresponsive to him, and he might feel hurt. Therefore, I always seek to avoid this possibility; but if I must, I choose not to hurt the Lord.

The Lord often quickens within me a chorus, *"When He calls I will answer."* This is the Lord telling me that He is about to knock on the door of my heart. Therefore, I am very careful about what I do, so I can remain sensitive to hear and respond to His voice.

The Manifest Presence of God

At times, this presence of the Lord may lead into a prolonged time of worship and communion with Him. Or, it may turn into intercession, which requires a turning inward to allow the burden to have its full outworking. It is important that we arrange our time so we can rightly respond, as the Lord may require.

While on a Pan-Am flight from New York to Datkar, I was sitting alone by a window. A lady across the aisle asked if I would change my seat and eat with her. But a short time before, I had felt this chorus rise up within, "*When He calls, I will answer.*" I had to tell her that I could not do this. Another man agreed and they talked all evening. I would have missed a very special time of communion with the Lord, during which He prepared me for the ministry that was before me.

The Lord may knock through a "*check of the spirit.*" This is an indication to stop whatever is being done and turn inward to listen for His voice. This has happened at home and my wife will say, "*Why are you so quiet?*" When I respond that I have something working in me, she immediately knows what I mean.

The Lord often speaks through alarm, or conviction, in a way that quickly arrests our attention. One year I had planned a stop in Baghdad to rest. I thought that while there, I would take a bus to the ancient city of Babylon. I woke in the morning with a presence and felt something alarming about it. I sat up in bed, and felt very uneasy in my spirit.

I said to the Lord, *"What is wrong?"* Suddenly before me stood the word "*Baghdad*." He never explained, but I knew at once that I was to remove that stop from my trip. Had I not obeyed, I might have become involved in some danger.

There is a price tag that is attached to this kind of walk. There have been times when I was with someone for dinner or visiting with them, and all of a sudden there came that nudge from the Lord, seeking my attention and I would have to excuse myself, and remove to a quiet place in order to respond.

I was visiting a family while teaching at a camp meeting. They had set out a very special meal for me. As we began to eat, suddenly that special nudge came in my spirit and I knew what it meant. As graciously as I possibly could, I excused myself and turned aside into the presence of the Lord. Later when I returned, the table was cleared and the food put away. I was never invited again.

There are times when the Lord asks that which is difficult for us.

While ministering in France, at the end of a service, a woman who may have been past ninety years of age, pushed a French coin into my hand. She said, *"You have helped me and I want to do something for you."* I knew she could not afford to give this coin, but I received it. The Lord had taught me long ago, *"I will command the ravens to sustain thee."* The ravens are God's ordinary nobodies.

The Lord had said to Elijah, *"I have commanded a widow woman to sustain you."* Elijah said to this woman, *"What do you have?"* She responded that she had some meal and a little flour and was going to make a pancake for herself and for her son, and then they would starve.

Elijah then said, *"First make me a cake."* I would like to ask Elijah, *"How did you feel when you asked that poor widow woman to give you her last cake, knowing the consequence?"* He was walking in obedience, therefore the Lord provided for the woman.

If I had refused to take that woman's coin, I would have deprived her of one of her greatest blessings from the Lord. But on my part, it took a humiliating experience. I had extra money with me, and this poor lady was giving me a small coin. Your obedience will kill you, but only then can the Lord raise you up.

There are those who do not understand my walk with the Lord. There is a price that must be paid, as friends may be lost. But I had made the determination that I would at all cost obey the Lord. It is not easy to keep such a commitment. The Lord may put our obedience to the test. We may be tempted to give in due to pressure from others, knowing that they do not understand.

In the Lord's time and way, He will vindicate us. In the meantime, the communion we have with Him cannot be compared to anything we might otherwise have.

Chapter 13

A Hearing Heart

"Behold, I stand at the door, and knock: If any man hear My voice, and open the door...."
"Revelation 3:20

This refers to both men and women; to anyone who will hear and respond. Some time ago, while I was in Australia, a Scripture in I Corinthians 14 was applied literally: *"The manifestation of the Spirit is given to every man."* Women were excluded and told they must remain silent. Rather, this speaks of *"opportunity."* The only condition is that we hear and respond, which will result in a feast with the Lord as He *"reveals"* Himself to us in His *"manifested presence."*

This *"experiencing"* of the Lord's manifested presence is available to all those who love the Lord, and demonstrate that love by their obedience. Its outworking will depend on how developed we are toward spiritual maturity, the Lord's purpose for our lives, our spiritual hunger and capacity, or, completely apart from us, the sovereign purposes of the Lord. Thus, it is not restricted to an isolated few or given because we are particularly holy.

We should rejoice when the Lord condescends to use us. If we ever think that we are special because the Lord is using us, remember the wonder that He has anything to do with us at all. If we become proud because we are being used by the Lord in any way, think of Balaam's donkey who prophesied to the prophet. If the Lord can use a donkey to speak, it is no great thing that He uses us.

His *"knocking"* on this doorway of spiritual opportunity indicates the Lord's singular desire to personally meet with us. Notice that the emphasis is on our *"hearing and responding."* Since this is the voice of the Lord knocking, *"spiritual perception and sensitivity"* is required for us to hear. Our *"capacity"* for spiritual perception can be increased in several ways - through teaching, by our feeding on the Word, by our fellowship with the Lord, and by prayer. It is very important that we seek to improve our ability to hear His voice

We should guard our *"spiritual awareness"* and never take this ability for granted. It is important that we never treat lightly the Lord's approach to us for fellowship. The Song of Solomon reveals a very high degree of intimacy between Solomon and the Lord. Yet toward the end of his life, Solomon turned so far from the Lord that his eternal state is left in doubt.

In Italy, there is a painting of Solomon, which shows him coming up in the resurrection before the Throne of God, in which the saved are on the right and the lost on the left. As Solomon approaches, there is an expression on his face, which indicates that he does not know if he belongs on the right or the left. There is one Scripture that gives a bit of a hope, where the Lord said to David, *"My mercy shall not depart from him."*

At the zenith of his seeking the Lord, the Lord appeared to Solomon in a dream and said, *"Ask what I shall give you."* Consider what your answer would be if the Lord were to say this to you. Our answer would be synchromatic with our true spiritual state, as it would reveal where we stand spiritually.

I can relate to this as I had a similar experience, but for a different purpose. Years ago, during a time of severe dealings, the Lord was grieved with me and took His Spirit from me for three days. Then after a time of severe disciplining, the Lord said, *"Ask what I shall give you,"* and I responded, *"There is only one thing I would ask, that I might have Your Spirit to return."*

Solomon's response was, *"Give me now wisdom."* In the Hebrew, the idea it carries is: *"Give your servant a hearing heart."* There are two types of hearing - the natural faculty of hearing through our physical ear, and the inner spiritual faculty of spiritual perception.

God is a Spirit and Psalm 94:9 tells us: *"He that planted the ear, shall He not hear? He that formed the eye, shall He not see?"* The Lord has no physical faculty of hearing, but rather, a spiritual faculty of hearing.

Because we have these two diverse ways to hear, we

tend to neglect our spiritual hearing. Therefore, Jesus emphasized our spiritual hearing, "*He that has an ear to hear, let him hear.*" They heard what Jesus was saying with their physical ear, but He reminded them that there is a much higher level of hearing by which we should hear. Only then can we know what He is really saying.

In John's messages to the seven Churches, he repeated to each of them, "*He that hath an ear, let him hear what the Spirit saith unto the Churches.*" This is an appeal to the inner hearing of the heart, which was the request of Solomon. When I retire at night, I often pray, "*Give now Thy servant a hearing heart.*" I am asking the Lord to help me to discern when He is knocking on the door of my heart, so I might respond.

Many times, I have been asked, "*How can I learn to better recognize the voice of the Lord?*" The best way is through our "*times of fellowship*" with the Lord. Comparing Himself to a shepherd, Jesus said:

> **"...The sheep follow Him: for they know His voice. And a stranger will they not follow, but will flee from him: for they know not the voice of strangers."**
> **John 10:4-5**

These sheep were not "*taught*" how to recognize the voice of their shepherd. Rather, they came to "*know*" his voice because they spent so much time with him. The time we spend waiting upon the Lord is tremendously important.

Along with this, we come to recognize the voice of the Lord through our spiritual experiences. The Holy Spirit will work with us and help us to learn the Lord's voice. Samuel is a good example of this. He had lain down to sleep and the Lord came and called Him. He ran to Eli thinking it was he who had called, but it was not. After he had come three times, Eli told him that it was the Lord who was calling him. Our translation says, *"the word of the Lord was not yet revealed to Samuel."* But the Hebrew reads, *"the voice of the Lord was not yet made known to Samuel."*

The best way to recognize His voice and leadings is by association. As we wait on the Lord and gain experience through our responses to His presence, we come to recognize and understand the voice of the Lord. A young child will usually cry when picked up by another. A newborn will not do this, but because the baby has spent much time with his mother, he has learned to recognize her.

If I were to spend time with you, you would come to recognize the sound of my voice. But if instead, someone explained to you the sound of my voice, it is most probable that you would not recognize it when I came into your presence.

There is no substitute for spending time in the presence of the Lord. As year by year, we grow spiritually, we will more easily recognize His voice.

Chapter 14

Those That Seek Me Early Shall Find Me

"Even the youths shall faint and be weary, and the young men shall utterly fall: But they that wait upon the Lord shall renew their strength; they shall mount up with wings like eagles; they shall run, and not be weary; they shall walk, and not faint."
Isaiah 40:30-31

Years ago, I stayed up until past midnight and then slept until late in the morning. The Lord let me know that this was to change, for I was to rise early each morning to meet with Him. The Lord further revealed that there is a deep inner satisfaction to be found in no other way, and a reward that is received when we spend time with Him early in the morning.

"I love them that love Me; and those that seek Me early shall find Me. That I may cause those that love Me to inherit substance; and I will fill their treasures."
Proverbs 8:17, 21

Throughout Church history, most all of those who left a mark upon the Lord's people knew the value of rising early in the morning to spend time with the Lord. The Word of God also affirms that the prophets of old rose early.

Although the Lord had made known to me that He desired to meet with me in the early morning hours, I had a very difficult time changing my sleep pattern. I would set the alarm for six o'clock, since I thought this was very early. When the alarm rang at six o'clock, I would push the button, turn over, and go back to sleep. Then after awhile, I did not even hear it when it rang. Finally I said to the Lord, "*This will never do, as I am unable to get up.*" I told the Lord that He would have to help me to get up.

The next evening, I asked the Lord to awaken me at six. I did not set the alarm, as I knew this had not worked. The next morning I was awakened out of a deep sleep by a blue jay that made a terrible racket, very close to my window. I got up to look for something to throw at it. Then I looked at the clock and realized that it was exactly 6 AM, and I was out of bed. But I got back in bed and went to sleep.

That night, I apologized to the Lord, asked Him to please wake me up at six the following morning, and that I would get up. At this time, I was staying with an elderly couple that was very nice and exceptionally quiet. The next morning I was awakened by a loud argument between the two, right outside my door. I looked at my clock, and it was exactly 6 AM, but again I went back to sleep.

The Manifest Presence of God

Once again that night, I asked the Lord's forgiveness and asked Him to wake me up at six o'clock the next morning. I was awakened by an automobile crash that was so loud that I jumped out of bed. I looked out the window, but could not see the cars, so again I went back to bed.

Again, I apologized and told the Lord that I was really ashamed of myself. I prayed, *"Lord, I will not ask You to wake me up again at six. Instead, Lord, I ask you to make me get up, and stay up."* The next morning, awakened with a terrible stomach pain, I ran for the bathroom. By the time I returned to the bed, I was wide-awake. I looked at my clock and again, it was exactly six o'clock.

Finally, I realized that the Lord was very determined that I was to get up at 6 AM to seek Him. From that time onward, I have always been careful to be in bed early enough in order to be up at six. It is of primary importance that we "promptly respond" when the Lord prompts us to come apart and wait upon Him.

To maintain an abiding walk in the presence of the Lord requires much self-discipline. Some years ago, I was teaching at a camp meeting. My wife was with me that year and we were together in the dining room for breakfast. I had ordered some pancakes and had asked for them to be made in a special way. The waitress seemed very pleased when she set them before me. As I sat looking at them, I felt a strong check in my spirit. My wife said, *"You are not supposed to eat this morning."* I responded that this was true, and she then said, "Then why are you sitting there, looking at them?" I felt embarrassed because they had been fixed special for me; but I left to go and wait on the Lord.

Being obedient to the Lord is not easy for any of us, but it is very important that we learn the value of "prompt obedience" in order to be available to Him. The Lord said to one of the prophets, *"When you go, do not enter into any house, or eat or drink with anyone."* The prophet was invited to eat and to rest, but he had to say no.

It is not easy for us to be obedient, knowing that others will not understand. This is the reason the Lord said, *"If anyone hears My voice, and opens the door."* This means that we may have to make changes in our plans in order to respond and be obedient.

> **"If you be willing and obedient, you shall eat the good of the land."**
> **Isaiah 1:19**

For example, some who have an intercessory ministry may be called by the Lord to come apart to pray while they are still washing the dishes. The temptation would be to hurry and finish, and then pray. If this is done, invariably, there will be no anointing for prayer or intercession. The opportunity would be missed, as there must be an *"immediate response."*

If any one of us were to go to the home of a friend and knock on their door, and then we noticed that they were ignoring our knock and continuing in whatever they were doing, we would feel hurt and leave. When they would finally respond, we would be gone and probably never again return.

This experience can be seen in the Song of Solomon.

> "I sleep, but my heart awakes; it is the voice of my Beloved that knocks, saying, Open to Me, My sister, My love, My dove, My undefiled: For My head is filled with dew, and My locks with the drops of the night."

> "I have put off my coat; how shall I put it on? I have washed my feet; how shall I defile them? My Beloved put in His hand by the hole of the door, and my bowels were moved for Him. I rose to open to my Beloved; and my hands dropped with myrrh, and my fingers with sweet smelling myrrh, upon the handles of the lock."

> "I opened to my Beloved; but my Beloved had withdrawn Himself, and was gone. My soul failed when He spoke: I sought Him, but I could not find Him; I called Him, but He gave me no answer." Song of Solomon 5:2-6

When the Bridegroom came and knocked on the door to her room, she had already retired, and she made excuses as to why she could not respond. Finally, when she decided to respond, he was gone, and that which was intended was missed.

> **"...I will come in to him, and sup with him, and he with Me."**
> **Revelation 3:20**

When we are obedient, not only will a need be met, but our prompt obedience will lead us into a time of intimate communion with the Lord. Because none of us easily come to this level of obedience, if we are sincere and truly desire His presence, there will be a progression in His dealings that will produce within us both the will and the ability to obey.

> **"Behold, I stand at the door, and knock...."**
> **Revelation 3:20**

This is the Lord's part. He lets us know that He desires our *"total attention,"* that we might *"enter into"* and *"experience"* His manifest presence.

"If anyone" This is our part. We are given the opportunity to choose to respond, which choice must be above all other things. *"Hears My voice"* If we are serious about personally knowing the Lord and having an ongoing relationship with Him, we must develop the ability to hear, or recognize His voice.

"And opens the door" The Lord will knock, but we must open the door and invite Him to come within.

"I will come in to him and sup with him, and he with Me."

Once we have invited the Lord to come within, we will find a satisfaction and fulfillment that can be experienced in no other way, as we "*commune*" with Him. We can easily see that this is a two way street, which requires an action on each side. Those who are wise will be "*prepared*" to arise early, "to enter" into His presence.

Chapter 15

To Him That Overcomes

"To him that overcomes will I grant to sit with Me in My throne, even as I also overcame, and am set down with My Father in His throne."
Revelation 3:21

This reveals the *"requirement"* for entering into a place of *"responsibility,"* in relation to the Lord's manifest presence.

To be in this *"throne relationship"* with the Lord, requires of us a quality of *"overcoming."* We must overcome our thoughts, our desires, and our natural abilities. This means that we have submitted the totality of our being to the Lord, and in our daily life experience, we are rising above the pulls of the earthly.

Thus, to be an overcomer requires that we make this major decision, followed by many lesser decisions, in submitting ourselves *"unconditionally"* to the Lord. Do we choose to give our priorities to the Lord, or do we give priority to our other interests? Our response, or our failure to respond, shows where our heart really is. It is here that we will fail, unless we recognize that the term "*over-coming*" involves both pressure and conflict.

In chapter one of Mark, the Lord did not speak to Peter and Andrew while they were resting, or when they were mending their nets. Rather, while they were casting their nets into the sea, He said, "*Come and follow Me.*" Seemingly, this was not the right time for the Lord to ask this. Peter could have said, "*Lord, I have just dropped my net into the sea and it will take awhile for the fish to get into it. As soon as I am done fishing, I will be with you.*"

But this is not what happened. The Word tells us that Peter straightway left the demands of his profession. He left his nets in the sea, fish and all, and followed Jesus. The Lord seeks for those who will respond in unquestioning, instantaneous obedience. If Peter had asked the Lord to wait until he had finished his fishing, the Lord would have gone on. Here, Peter's priorities were tested. His obedience had to overcome his professional interest.

By trade, I am a pattern draftsman. Both my grandfather and father were businessmen, which trait was imparted into my life at an early age. I received intensive training in Germany and then came to the United States at the age of twenty-one in 1925. Soon, I opened my own drafting office in New York City and worked long and hard, patterning drawings for the Patent Office in Washington.

I was alone in the office one Saturday afternoon when "*suddenly*," I heard a voice saying, "*Go down to the street and testify of Me.*" I thought, this is the Lord, but I am very busy and I must get this work done, as it has been promised by a certain time.

I had hardly started back to work when the power of God so moved on me that it literally shook the pencil out of my hand. After awhile this manifest power subsided, so I picked up my pencil and went back to work. I sometimes wonder why the Lord was so patient with me.

Again, the Lord said, "*Go down to the street and testify of me.*" I knew what He wanted, but again I said that I was too busy. And again, the power came down and literally shook the pencil out of my hand.

Finally, I came to understand that the Lord wanted me to put my work in second place and obey Him. I went down to the subway at Forty Second Street, and entered a subway car and began talking to the people who were near me about my experience of salvation. Then, I went from car to car testifying about the Lord.

As I entered a car toward the end of the train, a policeman was standing there. After I started speaking, I saw him scowling at me. Because I had to go past him to get to the next car, I became scared. In my heart I said, "*Lord, I have to walk past him, please make a way for me.*" Then I walked into the next car without a problem, and testified. After this, I left the train and went back to work in my office.

Four weeks later, the Lord spoke to me about going to Bible School. I was able to obey, even though I was very fond of my work and was doing well. Because there was a conflict within concerning my obedience, the Lord prepared me so I would be able to pass the test that I would face concerning the giving up of my business and going to Bible School.

Also, we may face conflicts in the social area of our lives. I was once engaged in a week of being separated to the Lord in fasting and prayer. My wife and small daughter were talking and I heard my daughter say, *"Mommy, doesn't daddy love us anymore?"* My wife said, *"He loves us. What makes you think that he doesn't?"* My daughter responded, *"He is always in there, and he never takes me for a walk."* I had a very hard time not giving up what I felt the Lord had instructed me to do, and take her for a walk. The pressure I felt was intense.

Another time, when I was very busy, the Lord prompted me to go into the attic because He desired to talk to me. I had a desk there so I could study or pray. I thought I would go up for a few minutes, and then I would be free to do what I needed to do.

I went up and said, *"Lord, here I am, what do you want?"* There was no response from the Lord. Again I said, *"Lord, I am available."* I waited, but the Lord said nothing. Then I said, *"Lord, will You hurry?"* Not a word. Then I said, *"Please, Lord, it is getting late."*

Finally, I realized that I must wait until "*I*" become quiet, as the Lord had something special to say. Then the Lord spoke three words to me, *"Desire spiritual gifts."* I knew that I was to write an article on this subject. I sat down at the table and began to write. The words came in a steady stream. I could hardly keep up until it was finished.

I had to overcome all that I felt urgently needed my attention. *"To him who overcomes"* - This means that other interests must be *"set aside"* at the beckoning of the Lord. Even legitimate things that bring us into a conflict with the Lord's interests, which seemingly cannot be put off.

In order for us to be in this *"overcoming"* relationship with Him, the Lord requires the *"right"* and the *"priority"* to our time. When He deals with us, we must overcome all other interests and activities. We must say *"no"* to things in order to say *"yes"* to Him. This may be very costly, as it cuts across all the human drives within us.

Although the price of saying yes to the Lord is great, the price of saying no is greater still. Gradually, we will learn that it will cost us far less to say *"yes"* to the Lord than to say *"no."* Only then will we become the overcomer whom the Lord will lift into His higher purpose.

Notice that there is a progression, which leads into the place where the Lord would have us.

"I stand and knock" Attention.

"If any man" Opportunity

"Hear" Perception

"My voice" Recognition

"And open the door" Response

"I will come into him" Communion

The *"manifest presence"* of the Lord is available to those who will respond in obedience to His desire to commune with them.

"Come, My beloved, let us go forth into the field; let us lodge in the villages. Let us get up early to the vineyards; let us see if the vine flourish, whether the tender grape appear, and the pomegranates bud forth: there will I give you My loves."

Song of Solomon 7:11-12

Now, we are ready to enter into a cooperative relationship with our Lord - "*let us go* (*together*)." Apart from His manifest presence in our lives, nothing else will ever satisfy or be fulfilling. We were created for this.

Bonus Chapters

These two Bonus Chapter were live messages by Walter H. Beuttler that were transcribed by Pearl Ray for the edification of the Body of Christ. All scriptures are from the KJV except where noted. 2) This message has been transcribed word for word (from Beuttler's own teachings) as accurately as possible (due to the quality of the recording). 3) Beuttler had his own dictionary of favorite words he used throughout his messages, and they have been transcribed and spelled out accordingly. 4) Spelling on certain proper names, airports, hotels, locations, etc. may not be exact. 5) Messages were spoken late 1960's, early 1970's. 6) Beuttler was a Bible teacher at NBI (a.k.a. EBI, Eastern Bible Institute) for 32 years traveling worldwide since early 1950's until a year before he went to be with the Lord in 1974.]

Bonus Chapter 1

Laws Governing the Presence

> "Now therefore, I pray thee, if I have found grace in thy sight, shew me now thy way, that I may know thee, that I may find grace in thy sight; and consider that this nation is thy people. And he said, My presence shall go with thee, and I will give thee rest."
> Exodus 33:13-14

The presence of God brings rest.

Now I want to make a few comments first on the matter of the knowledge of God. In

Jeremiah 24:7, God said to Jeremiah:

"I will give them an heart to know me."

Please do not think that I am anti-education or anti-knowledge. Only a fool would do that. Do try to understand what I try to say, and it is this: that _in the_ *final analysis, the true knowledge of God is a matter of the heart much more than it is a matter of the head*. We need to be informed; we need to be well informed, no question about that, but *the true knowledge of God simply does not come by mere information*. I said, "*mere*," I didn't say information, I said, "*mere*." We need that information, but in the final analysis, *the true knowledge of God is a matter of experience.*

What I see here and have felt for years is this, that in our Bible schools, there is a paramount need, and that need is that our students, sometime or another, have a personal encounter with a personal God. All our book learning is ever so valuable, but it cannot take the place of a personal experience where we personally meet God and come face to face, so to speak, and have a personal encounter.

I had that in CBI when I was in my last year. I had a wonderful time with God throughout the Bible school career. I didn't fool my time away like the rest. I sought the Lord. I was in this country all alone with nobody to help me. It was sink or swim, that was all, either Beuttler had to sink or swim. Well, I swam; at least tried to.

Graduation neared and I didn't know where to go after graduation. I had no home, no relatives, no close friends. I didn't want to be a burden. A few weeks before the end of school, a student walked into my room, a big husky fellow.

He said, "*Walter, where are you going to go after graduation?*" I answered, "*I don't know.*"

He asked, "*Are you going to go west?*" "*I don't know,*" I said.

"Are you going to go east?" he asked. I still answered, *"I don't know."*

He then asked, *"Do you think you'll be a pastor?"* *"I don't know,"* I answered.

"You might be an evangelist?" *"I don't know."*

He said, *"Man, what do you know?"*

I said, *"Well, I guess I don't know anything."*

Then he straightened up, brought his chest out and said, *"Boy, I'm glad I'm not like you."* And I still see that disdaining wave of his hand, *"My father is the superintendent of the Kansas district"* - which was correct - *"and he's also the personal friend of the general superintendent in Springfield. Boy, when I get out of school, I don't have to start at the bottom like you fellows. I'll be starting at the top. My father's going to give me a church, and it's going to be a good one. Boy, I'm glad I'm not like you."*

And he walked out of the room and shut the door with a bang, and the full impact got into my heart. I felt awful and said, *"I guess he's right. Where will I go? What will I do?"* I knew I had a call, but that's all I knew.

I dropped down on my knees at my cot (they weren't big, just a cot), pointed my thumb toward the door and said, *"Father, did You hear what he said?"*

All of a sudden, like the bat of an eye, the snap of a finger, God gave me a revelation. It came like this (he snapped his finger), and I had the whole thing. You have to accept that, or understand it or not understand it; I can't change it.

This is what the implication was of that personal encounter. I have to put it in words, but the whole thing came all at once. It was as though God were speaking, "*It is true that his father is the superintendent of a district. It is furthermore true that his father is the personal friend of the general superintendent of Springfield. But it is also true that I am the superintendent of all superintendents including the superintendent of Springfield, and I am your superintendent.*"

In other words, He was the super superintendent.

I turned around, because I had moved to sitting on the cot, and I turned around and dropped back on my knees and said, "*Father, from this day, I'm making You my personal superintendent.*" And He has been a good one.

That was an encounter where God and I, so to speak, came face to face and it has been the backbone of my ministry ever since. I have credentials in my pocket, but they are not my basic credentials. I have credentials from Him.

Would you like to know what happened? About a week before graduation (only a short time later), I got a letter from a pastor on Long Island. How come? I don't know.

"*Brother Beuttler, If you don't know where to go or what to do after graduation, come east and give us a week of meetings."*

Apparently my superintendent went to His phone right away and called up Long Island to let this pastor know to write Beuttler a letter. I was there and the pastor said, *"Brother Beuttler, the people would like you to stay another week. Could you?"*

"Sure could," I answered.

Next week a pastor walked in and said, *"Brother Beuttler, where are you going next week?"*

I said, *"No place."*

He said, *"Could you come to my church?"* *"Yes,"* I said.

"All right, that's good," he said.

I stayed a week and he asked, *"Could you stay another week?"* *"Yes,"* I answered.

Next week another pastor walked in, *"Where are you going next week?"* *"I don't know - no place,"* I answered.

He asked, *"Could you come to my church?"*

That was in 1931 and it's been going on ever since, that is to say, God has opened doors all the way down to this very day. *I had a personal encounter with a personal God, and that encounter has lasted to this very date.*

My heart is in Bible school work, you understand that, and *I am greatly concerned that students have a personal encounter*, something like Ezekiel had, we'll say in principle. He said, **"The heavens were opened and I saw visions of God."**

Now it's one thing to have an *open* library and an *open* encyclopedia, and I despise neither libraries nor encyclopedias as I'm a student by nature, but *we need more than an open encyclopedia. We individually need an open heaven where we come in personal contact with God and receive something from God for our own lives.* Don't carry this on into the visionary now. I'm not talking about visions; I'm talking about a personal encounter with God in some way.

So often students now get a vision of Shakespeare, of Plato, of Socrates, what have you. It has its place, but *in this work, a primary importance is a personal revelation of a personal God in our hearts.*

"I will give them a heart to know me."

Thank God for all the information. We can acquire useful information, but it will not carry the ball in the ministry. You can know all about different subjects, and I'm sure you've heard this from others. But in the final analysis, it's what we've got from God in here (pointing to heart) that is going to carry the ball for us, much more our personal relationship to Him than what we have acquired by way of knowledge, though I certainly do not despise that by any means.

What I'm talking about is a personal encounter with God, and that is a matter of the heart. I've had numbers of encounters, but we have no time, and it's not necessary to explain.

I'd like to touch on Matthew 11 for a moment to point out to you a truth there that I think is quite pertinent.

"At that time Jesus answered and said, I thank thee, Oh Father, Lord of heaven and earth, because *thou hast hid these things from the wise and prudent, and hast revealed them unto babes*. Even so, Father; for so it seemed good in they sight." Matthew 11:25-26

Do you notice here that there are things, truths, which God deliberately withholds from some people? Jesus had just been teaching and then He said, **"Father, I thank you that you hid these things from the wise and prudent, and hast revealed** (disclosed them, shared them) **unto babes."** <u>There are truths which God deliberately withholds from some people, and deliberately shares those very truths with others</u>. Withholds from whom? Jesus said, **"The wise and the prudent."**

That raises a question, *"Who are the wise and the prudent?"* Some think the educated, but I don't think so. I don't think God has anything against good, sound education in its place. I don't think so at all.

What you have here is an expression that refers to *the smart alexes*. There are no smart alexes here, but we've had them in NBI - *The intellectual snobs.* They come to class and know more than the teacher. Maybe sometimes they do in some points. I have learned some things from students. But there are people who think they know everything. The fact is that they know so little; they don't know enough to know that there is more to know. The more you know, the more you know how little you know in comparison to what there is still to be known. <u>The more we enlarge the circle of our knowledge, the more we enlarge the awareness of how much there still is that we do not know</u>.

To Einstein was said, "*My, you know a lot.*" He answered, "*I don't know anything.*"

That was Einstein! Well, what did he mean? That man knew so much that he knew enough to know there is so much more he didn't know, that what he did know was very, very small in comparison to what he didn't know. *The more we know the humbler we ought to get.*

Here we have *the conceited, the snobs, the know-it-alls, the unteachables, the critics*, and the Lord says, "*All right Father, I thank you that you have hid these truths from the snobs.*"

Now people who are uneducated can be snobs too. I don't think that has anything to do here with education. *It has to do with an attitude, a critical, snobbish, know-it-all attitude.*

"Hast revealed them unto babes."

Who are the babes? I would say *the humble, the simple, the open, the responsive, the hungry, the uncritical babes.*

The Manifest Presence of God

Have you ever watched a mother nurse her baby? Does a 4 week old baby say, *"Hey Mom, before I drink this white stuff I want a chemical analysis? I want to know the proportion of fat and protein, water and phosphorus."* No, the baby just goes to work. God, at creation, has put something in there, and the baby just goes to work and drinks it. *Oh God, give us simplicity*, and I don't mean we should be simpletons. **"Prove all things, hold fast that which is good,"** but that's a different subject. We're dealing with another area now.

Do you know we can be so analytical with truth, that with our over analysis, we destroy the truth? Yes sir!

You go into the area of the presence of God and try to analyze everything: *"Now what is the difference between the awareness of His presence and His omnipresence"* (or what have you)? You can go and try to divide there, and before you know it, you've torn the real truth up and lost the experience. There are some ramifications I do not pursue because the farther they are pursued, the more you destroy the thing.

Last summer I was walking along the street in Bangkok, Thailand. I think it was providential, although I wouldn't want to affirm that. I was walking along to the Siam Hotel from the hotel where I stayed because I liked the Siam better for eating. On my way I found my favorite flower in the Far East, the lotus. It was lying on the side, a nice purple, cup-shaped lotus. Don't ask me how it got there. I can only think somebody carried a bunch of those flowers and lost one. Anyhow, I found it.

The lotus interests me very much and I thought, "*I'm going to take this thing and analyze it.*" I took it and opened up the petals and looked on the inside, and what a beautiful symmetrical arrangement. It was just delightful to examine. I broke the thing apart, cut it apart, looked here and there. What a marvelous, marvelous organism you have there. I found out what I had wanted to know, some of it anyhow. Some I still don't understand. *But when I got done, I had no lotus. I had pieces. I knew a little more than I did before, but I had no lotus. We can carry analogies so far that we destroy the flower, destroy the truth. We know more and have less.* Do with that what you like.

Turning back now, particularly in this matter of the presence of God. Someone asked me on the way back the other night, "*Brother Beuttler, what are you going to do when you don't have the presence of God?*"

At the time I didn't want to discuss it because I was weary and thought I'd get back into the subject again in another meeting. Now here again we have a theological difficulty, but I leave it alone. There is such a thing as the awareness, a consciousness, a sense of the reality of the presence of God, but when somebody says, "*Well, what do you do when you don't have the presence?*"

Uh! Well, I wouldn't put it that way, I would say, "*What would you do when you don't*

'feel' the presence?" There's a big difference, you know, between *feeling the presence* and *having the presence*, so I would change the question and say, "*What do you do when*

you don't 'feel' the presence?" That's very simple. I praise God for the presence, still I fall back on the Book, **"I will never leave thee nor forsake thee"** and **"Do not I fill heaven and earth."** God is with me and with you just as much when you don't feel His presence as when you do feel it. You see, you go right back into the Word, **"I will never leave thee nor forsake thee."**

Like we said this morning, *"And thy Father which is in secret."* I don't have to feel His presence to believe He is in secret. The Lord loves to do things for us. I think I better take you to John 14:21. You know the Lord's a great lover.

"He that hath my commandments, and keepeth them, he it is that loveth me: and he that loveth me shall be loved of my Father, and I will love him, and will manifest myself to him." John 14:21

Now here you have *a unique love.* In this verse, the love of the Father for you and me is *conditional*; *it is based on our loving Him*: *"Those who love me, I will love,"* the implication being, *"Those who don't love me, I won't love."*

Now here we have to rightly divide the word of truth, of course. **"God so loved the world that He gave."** God loves all humanity without prior condition, and yet here it says, **"He that hath my commandments, and keepeth them, he it is that loveth me: and he that loveth me shall be loved of my Father."** So here is something unique. What you have here is this: In the first place, <u>our love for Him is not proven by what we say, but by what we do.</u>

"I love Him," but that doesn't prove anything. *Our love is proven by our obedience.* That's what He says, **"He that hath my commandments, and keepeth them: he's the one that loves me."** "*If he loves me by keeping My commandments, the Father will love him and I will love him.*"

This has nothing to do with the general love of God for all people. This is somewhat of a lover relationship. *The Father and the Son will reciprocate our love for Him as demonstrated by obedience.* What He does here, He tells us, "*I will give such a one the tokens, the reciprocation of My love for him by means of, and will manifest Myself to him.*"

I do my studying with different translations. I think I have about two dozen or so different translations that I use. I found this word "*manifest*" most interesting. You have translations like this:

"I will *make myself real* to him;" "I will *disclose myself* to him;"

"I will *make myself known* unto him;" "I will *show myself* to him;"

"I will *plainly show myself* to him."

I know what this is, for I've seen the Lord on two or three occasions. Once in response to fasting and prayer for a week, but I can't go into that.

If you take the Pulpit Commentary (I think it's the

Pulpit Commentary), and check on this verse, it says that this word "*manifest*" in the Greek is so strong as to mean *nothing less than a manifestation of the Lord perceivable by our physical senses.* You can check on this yourself. I've had the experience, so I'm very much assured of it. *Here the Lord will give us tokens of appreciation for our appreciation of Him.*

Down at school around 1950, the Lord had given me a tremendous hunger to seek Him. I had that many years before, but didn't follow through, but then it came back. I sought the Lord in between all my schoolwork. Schoolwork is heavy, and I'm out in ministry all the time. Every weekend I'm somewhere. Still, I sought the Lord in every crack of time I had, especially by night. I get up during the night, many times in the middle of the night for no other reason than to seek Him, to worship Him, to sit in His presence (*unfelt* presence), simply sit there. That went on for some time, then the Lord began to reveal Himself.

One night, He walked into our cottage. I heard Him step by step as He moved through the cottage; heard Him turn around and then spoke to me in an audible voice. On one of those nights, I was sitting there simply admiring Him. I got up about 2:30 admiring Him, keeping Him company. I said, "*Lord, so many of Your people are asleep now, and I want to get up to spend a little time with You to keep You company.*"

I had the clearest perception of the Lord walking toward me from behind. I didn't see Him, but had the perception of it. It was as real as could be. I perceived Him bending over me from behind, and literally felt a sensation of drops falling on top of my head. I instinctively knew this sensation was the teardrops of His appreciation for somebody that would get up in the middle of the night for no other reason than to keep Him company. Now that happened only once, tokens of His appreciation. The Lord loves to do that.

Now God hears what I say. I had sought the Lord for hours upon hours during the night, deprived myself of sleep. *I wanted Him*. I sought no experience, simply Him, out of a great hunger, when one night I was awakened by a man singing, a man's voice singing in my bedroom. It woke me up; the voice awakened me, and there stood the Lord by the window, full size, in white garments, looking my way, singing two stanzas for me a song that I had never heard before or since. And then He was gone.

"I will manifest myself to him; I will disclose myself to him; I will show myself to him, I will plainly show myself to him."

This is a wonderful thing we're getting into here, I mean the experience.

Different people have different attitudes. Some love to hear me speak that way; some hate to hear me say it. Different people take a different attitude, but I just do my knitting. Anybody that likes it can like it; anybody that wants to lump it can lump it. I know what it is; I was there.

Do you remember in Genesis 3:8?

The Manifest Presence of God

"And Adam and Eve hid themselves from the presence of the Lord."

Now I think they made, a very transparent excuse when God made inquiry, *"Well Lord, you know we forgot to wear our bikini."* Now I will get in trouble! I don't think that was their real reason. There could be differences of opinion, and I don't argue. I just share and go on. I think the real reason was, at least the basic reason was, that *they were no longer in a right relationship with God. They had a sense of guilt.* Believe you me, <u>when we have a sense of guilt because of transgression, it is very, very hard to be comfortable in the presence of God</u>. There is an instinctive urge to shy away from the presence of God. A bad conscience, guilt, is not a comfortable thing in the presence of God. *I think they hid themselves more from guilt than the other reason.*

There are some people today who have no use for the presence of God, and I would not be a bit surprised if, in many cases, there is something, somewhere out of harmony with the holiness of God. Such people simply feel uncomfortable in God's presence, and so to speak, hide themselves.

In Genesis 4:16 we read,

"And Cain went out from the presence of the Lord, and dwelt in the land of Nod, on the east of Eden.

Actually, as you know, he was sent out. *He was not allowed to remain in the presence of the Lord because he slew his brother.*

Today Christians do not kill their brother or their sister

with a knife, *but we can do it with the tongue. We have to be so very careful what our tongues say about other people, because sooner or later, it will cost us the presence of God. Using our tongue maliciously against God's other children, however seemingly justified our argument might be, is not compatible with maintaining the presence of God.*

Cain slew his brother.

I learned a hard lesson when I was a young pastor. A lady in the church was talking about me. She was dead wrong, and I won't take time to explain, as I want to use the time elsewhere. I thought, "*Well, she's talking about me, I'll talk about her…bla…bla…bla…bla,*" which of course, was the wrong thing.

The Lord gave me a dream.

In the dream, I stood behind the pulpit. My tongue came out of my mouth about a foot long. It came to a sharp point. I also saw a hand with a pair of scissors in it that were opened. The hand with the scissors came over my tongue and clipped it off. It dropped on the platform, and there it still kept going, wiggling, yapping away. I woke up and knew God was speaking. I knew what He meant, "*Beuttler, you need your tongue cut off.*"

Believe you me, I took heed and kept still. *Cain lost the presence of God. He was sent out because he slew his brother.*

"But Jonah rose up to flee unto Tarshish from the presence of the Lord." Jonah 1:3

The Manifest Presence of God

Jonah ran in disobedience. He ran away. You cannot flee from God's omni-presence. What did David say, **"If I go to the uttermost parts of the earth, you are there."**

There is no escape from the omnipresence of God, but there is an escape from a certain relationship that we have with God, an awareness of His presence, that I, for myself, cherish so greatly; that wondrous presence, comforting, soothing, and assuring. It is so enjoyable and I love it.

We find David valued God's presence in Psalms 51:11,

"Cast me not away from thy presence."

David here valued the presence of God and did not want to lose it. *I myself am trying to be very careful that I do not lose the awareness of God's presence.*

I lost it one year in Europe. The Lord asked me to go to Berlin, and I wouldn't go. I came from Africa, had to go to Iceland, and I said, *"Lord, I'm not stopping in Berlin. I'm tired. I have had enough traveling."* I wouldn't go. Whew! Did God ever get after me! *I felt like God was "a million miles away."* He left me out in the cold, and I had some time to get the awareness of that presence back because it was *willful disobedience* to the leading of His Spirit.

Psalms 16 says, **"In thy presence there is fullness of joy."**

There are those that rejoice in the presence of God. Now I would like to come to the aspects of this presence.

Briefly, I'll take Psalms 71:3:

"Be thou my strong habitation, whereunto I may continually resort." Psalms 71:3

Although the word presence is not used here, the thought is there. *David used the presence of the Lord as a resort. You know what a resort is. It's a place where you go to for refreshing, for relaxation, for rest, for recuperation.*

I have resorts all over the world where I go to in my travels. If I don't, I can't keep up the ministry. I have places where I go one day, two days, maybe three days. *Nobody knows where I am*. It's a resort. In Thailand it's Hat Yai Beach; in Hong Kong, it's Macau down the South China coast a bit, 4 hours steamboat from Hong Kong; and other areas of the world where I go for a little retreat, to be all alone, quiet. Nobody asks you, *"Where did Cain get his wife?"* (It's an easy question to answer. Obviously, he married his sister.)

It's a resort where you get recuperated. As far as I'm concerned, *I use the presence of God for the same thing.* I go about, a sense of the presence of God steals over me. I got it the other day in Rochester. I went over to get some travel business done, and had a nice presence there. I was walking on Main Street or something, had a presence steal over me, so I went down to the Holiday Inn. I know they have nice, comfortable chairs and nobody bothers you. I just sat there, *"Hallelujah."* (under his breath). *It was a resort. It's an oasis in the desert. I don't know what I would do without it.*

Students, *I would recommend to you the awareness of the*

presence of God as a resort, as an oasis to which you can flee and recuperate in His presence.

Students, *we've got to walk straight in this kind of a thing.*

Down in Buenos Aires, I stayed in the suburb with a missionary, and had to take a train downtown to a rail station, the subway across town to Constitution Square, take another train out about 40 minutes where we had our Bible school. I had my ticket all the way, but there was no conductor, so when I got there and came back, I had a completely valid ticket. They're useable both ways. I didn't say, "*Hallelujah! The Lord knows how to supply your needs. He didn't let the conductor come and pinch the ticket. Glory! I got another ticket.*" Oh no, I went to the ticket office, there was a trash box, and I took a good ticket, tore it up, threw it into the trash can and bought another one. In the natural, people would say, "*What a dumb fool,*" but not so. *Who can stand this presence? We have to go straight with this thing.* (I'll also boil this down without boiling it up!)

In Psalms 15:1, David asked a question, **"Lord, who shall abide in thy tabernacle? Who shall dwell in thy holy hill?"**

Different translations read differently. For instance: **"Who shall consort with thee?"** I like that! *Who will be your consort? Who shall find a home in the presence of God?*

You see folkses, *the presence of God is my home all over the world. I take this home with me. I don't know what I would do without it. Wherever I go, I want that presence.*

Now David answers the question,

"He that walketh uprightly (a reference to the feet), **and worketh righteousness** (a reference to the hand), **and speaketh the truth in his heart** (a reference to the tongue as well as to the heart). **He that backbiteth not with his tongue** (again the tongue), **nor doeth evil to his neighbor, nor taketh up a reproach against his neighbor** (a reference to the ear). **In whose eyes a vile person is contemned; but he honoureth them that fear the Lord. He that sweareth to his own hurt, and changeth not. He that putteth not out his money to usury, nor taketh reward against the innocent. He that doeth these things shall never be moved."** Psalms 15:2-5

Here is a reference to the feet, where they walk; to the hands, what they do; to the tongue, what it speaks; to the ears, what they pick up; a reference to the eyes, what they behold.

Now really, David is saying, *"Who shall find a home in the presence of God? Who shall consort with thee? Who will be the guest of God?"*

And *there are laws that govern the presence of God. There are laws that govern our faculties: that govern our feet, where they walk; laws that govern our hands, what they do; laws that govern our eyes, what they behold.*

There is no room for pornography, not in the presence of God. That's out. It's out anyhow, of course.

The Manifest Presence of God

There's a reference to the tongue in what it says. There's no room for foul, dirty, off-color language.

There are laws of the presence of God that govern the tongue. There's no room for smut. There are laws that govern the ears; that do not lend themselves to gossip.

I was on a field riding with a missionary, and he came to a red light. While he was there, a woman walked up rapidly, spoke to him and spilled the beans. I won't explain what beans they were, but they weren't navy beans. That missionary was all flustered. The light changed, but she held him. I sat there and couldn't help but hear what she said. Finally he went. He said, *"Brother Beuttler, did you hear that?"*

I said, *"I couldn't help it, but don't worry. I'll never take it home."* And I never did. He would not be a missionary today. He's a good missionary, but he fell into something. She spilled the beans. I kept my mouth shut. I don't tell on people. You'd be surprised what I run into.

Before the Lord sent me away, the Lord gave me some special training on how to travel for Him. Included was a passage from Isaiah 42,

"Seeing many things, but thou observeth not; hearing many things, but he heareth not."

In other words, *"Beuttler, don't see, pay no attention, don't pick up any reproaches."*

One year Springfield said to me, *"Brother Beuttler, we're

having trouble on such and such a field. Will you keep your ears open and bring back a report and tell us what you find." I found out all right without looking. I don't snoop, but some things you just run into. I never wrote. The man from Springfield visited us at home and said, *"Brother*

Beuttler, you never gave us a report. Why not?"

I said, *"The Lord sent me to teach not to report."* And I never told them what I found out.

It's a wonderful thing to keep your mouth shut.

There are laws that govern His presence, govern our faculties, that we need to conform to. Believe you me, a traveling man has a thousand and one ways to go wrong if he wants to. *It's a mighty good thing to know the laws that govern the presence of God.* Of all the opportunities that come your way in a summer's ministry - all kinds. These laws govern in Bible school. *We have to do it straight, be honest, be on the level.*

Down at school we had a snow, and a pretty head was looking out of the upper window - a she head, I mean. A fellow takes a snowball and sends it up to that head. The head ducked and the snowball went through the window and hit the other one, and nobody did it.

The dean of men wanted to know, *"Who messed up the wall? Who broke the window?"* They were all saints!

"Do you know who it was?" he asked. *"No,"* they all said.

The Manifest Presence of God

"*Well, it was one of you fellows.*" "*It wasn't me.*"

The law of the presence would require that when a student does damage to the building, he ought to go to the office, make the fact known, and after school make repairs and pay on the spot. Don't look at me so mad. That's the law of the presence.

There are laws that govern our feet, where they walk; our hands, what they do; our tongue, what it says; our heart, what it thinks; our eyes, what they're allowed to behold; our ears, what they pick up.

"He that doeth these things shall never be moved."

In other words, *there are laws of the presence of God that govern our human faculties. If we want to be the Lord's consort, and He ours; and we want to find a home in the presence of God* (not merely an occasional visit, but an abiding presence), *we must comply with the laws, which govern the home of the presence of God.*

I suppose you have rules like we have rules.

We had a girl come in one year with a big bushel head and said, "*Where is my telephone?*

Where is the carpeting in my room?"

The dean of women said, "*There isn't any.*" "*Where is my private bathroom?*"

"*Well, we haven't got any.*" "*What kind of a place is this?*" "*That's the place that is.*"

"I think that I shall go home right away."

And the dean of women said, *"That would be a good idea. I agree with you, miss."* She had no intention of complying with the laws of the home.

If we do not have any intention to comply with the laws of the home of the presence of God, we will not have His abiding presence. We might have an occasional visit, but we will not have that abiding presence.

"He that doeth these things shall never be moved."

He shall never have to vacate the home of the presence of God.

"Show me now thy way, that I may know thee."

And again may the Lord be able to say to every one of us,

"My presence shall go with thee, and I will give thee rest."

These are some of the fragments of the laws on *maintaining* a home in the presence of God.

Bonus Chapter 2

Four Ways to Lose God's Presence

I felt that I would like to point out to you and comment a bit on four ways of losing God's presence. I'll enumerate them for you first so you'll know which way we're going, and then I'll go back to each one.

1) Loss of our consecration;

2) Disobedience;

3) Substitution;

4) Neglect.

I am not suggesting there aren't any others, but these are four we are going to use based on the Word of God.

Turning first of all to the Book of Judges 16:4-5, 16-20.

"And it came to pass afterward, that he loved a woman in the valley of Sorek, whose name was Delilah. And the lords of the Philistines came up unto her, and said unto her, Entice him, and see wherein his great

strength lieth, and by what means we may prevail against him, that we may bind him to afflict him; and we will give thee every one of us eleven hundred pieces of silver." Judges 16:4-5

Obviously, these Philistines valued Samson. Otherwise, they would not have paid such an immense sum in order to get at his strength.

"And it came to pass, when she pressed him daily with her words, and urged him, so that his soul was vexed unto death; that he told her all his heart, and said unto her, There hath not come a razor upon mine head; for I have been a Nazarite unto God from my mother's womb; if I be shaven, then my strength will go from me, and I shall become weak, and be like any other man. And when Delilah saw that he had told her all his heart, she sent and called for the lords of the Philistines, saying, Come up this once, for he hath showed me all his heart. Then the lords of the Philistines came up unto her, and brought money in their hand. And she made him **sleep upon her knees; and she called for a man, and she caused him to shave off the seven locks of his head; and she began to afflict him, and his strength went from him. And she said, The Philistines be upon thee, Samson. And he awoke out of his sleep and said, I will go out as at other times before, and shake myself. And he wist not that the Lord was departed from him."** Judges 16:16-20

All of us, I think, know the story of Samson. Notice here this word **"enticed."** She enticed him and got him into a place where the man told her all his heart. Basically, what we have here is this:

Samson lost the secret of his consecration.

He was a Nazarite. As a Nazarite, he had to meet certain conditions. He could not drink wine; he could not eat grapes; he could not eat raisins - not even raisin pie; he had to let the locks of his hair grow, and in those days, that was a reproach, a sign of reproach. A Nazarite had to bear reproach for the Lord's sake.

This Delilah so pressed upon this man that finally he gave away the secret of his power. Now there are things I do not understand. Why did this man trifle with the secret of his power? She said, **"Samson, the Philistines be upon thee."** Then she did it a second time, and she did it a third time. Why that man did not come to his senses, I don't know. Perhaps the man was so overwrought that the man, in spite of the fact that he saw he was gravitating toward trouble, could not muster sufficient strength to get out of that place and run for his life. He played along and played along; he gravitated toward disaster.

About a year or two ago I watched a movie on Samson and Delilah on TV. I've often seen it advertised over the years, but I don't go to the movies, but when they showed it on TV, I thought, *"I'll just see what this is all about."*

I was amazed at the reproduction of the times in those days. It was an education of the times in which this story took place. They showed how Samson was finally robbed of his power. Eventually he was pulling at the mill and the lords of the Philistines were laughing and drinking, making fun over Samson.

Delilah stood by, and you actually could tell she was very remorseful after what she had done. Here was the king of the Philistines, and other kings had come and laughed about Samson. Delilah stood not far away and said to this king, *"Well, your army has finally conquered Samson."*

The king said very gravely, *"No, my army didn't, you did."*

That thing was so impressive. I'll never forget it. An army of warriors could not defeat

Samson; she did.

You know as well as I do that many a ministry has been wrecked, many a home broken up by a similar enticement. They are all over and all over the world. It seems that Satan is especially anxious to get at the ministry if he possibly can, because if he can drag down a minister, he's going to drag down many other people who have put their confidence in him. These Delilah's are all over.

I sat in Rio de Janeiro at the sidewalk café drinking what they call down there a guala naught, a sharp drink made from berries. I like it very much. I was just sitting there. A lady walked along, and she spotted me, because you know, an American stands out like a sore thumb. An American is recognized anywhere.

She walked up and said, *"How do you do, Mr. American?"*

"Fine," I answered. I knew right away what was up. Don't

you kid yourself. I'm no fool. I knew right away what she was after, but I played along and said, *"Fine."*

"How do you like Rio de Janeiro?" she asked. *"Fine,"* I said.

"Been here before?" "Oh yes, many times." "Are you alone?" "Yes."

"Are you married?" "Yes."

"Are you staying at a hotel?" "Yes."

"Which one?"

I said, *"Oh, now wait a minute, lady. Here is where we stop. How about it?"*

She said, *"Oh, I thought maybe you were lonesome and I could keep you company for a night."*

I said, *"No, I'm not lonesome, and I don't need company - not with you."*

Those things happen all the time and many, many a minister has stories to tell along these lines. But students, *we need to watch our consecration.* Our consecration may not be lost just along these lines. There are other lines, but let's look at Samson.

Here was Samson, and they took the secret of his power from him. Now notice: he said, **"I will go out as at other times before and shake myself."** Well, he shook himself, and his shook was an empty shook. He went through the same format, the same formula, **"I'll shake myself,**

and *he wist not that the Lord was departed from him.*"

I would say we have here - the suggestion at least - that *it's possible to lose the presence without knowing it until it is needed*. We Pentecost can get into the format, hanging onto mere formulas, *without actually having the power to effect any results*.

When I was seeking the Baptism, I was under the power lying on the floor. You know we used to have that in Pentecost. I haven't seen it in many years. I know there were days when the power of God shook people, knocked them off their seats down on the floor. I've had it many times. We've had it in school in the earlier days, not recent years.

These two ladies worked on me. They wanted to give me the Baptism. Well, they had a lot of *"shook,"* but nothing in their *"shook."* One pounded my chest: bang, bang, bang, bang, *"Bring it up, brother, bring it up, bring it up,"* bang, bang, bang, bang. I wish I had: my supper, that is, bring it up. I didn't want to bring anything up, I wanted to be filled.

One of them took hold of my Adam's apple, began to look for it and squeeze around my throat and said, *"Brother, now say, Ga, ga, ga, ga, goo, goo, goo, goo."*

I felt like saying, *"Cock a doddle do o o o o!"*

They were shouting tongues in my ear; they rubbed me; they massaged me; they did everything. Finally, I was so disgusted, I got up and walked home. I know what they were trying to do, but I don't know what they thought.

You know God may have uses for the laying on of hands with the power of God flowing through our hands healing people, baptizing people. I have seen ministers go through what they used to have, "*Hallelu ug ug ug ug,*" and what have you, and it's a bunch of blub, blub, blub, blub.

Once there was the power, now there is the shake, the form, the format. <u>We can lose the presence without being aware of it</u>. <u>We will surely lose it by losing our consecration, the secret of His presence</u>.

Let's go to I Samuel 16:14, and here I'll need a little more time perhaps. Here is something tragic. The other is tragic too.

Maybe I should add something. It came to mind, but I thought to bypass it. I had a very godly pastor, and he said to me, "*Brother Beuttler, the devil tries to get the ministry anyway he can.*"

He told me this story:

I was sitting in my study with the door open toward the street. It was a hot day. A woman came in to get some counseling. (You know, there's a great place for counseling, but counseling sessions can be extremely dangerous.) And she came for counseling, and lo and behold, she jumped up, sat on his lap, put her arm around his neck and said, "*Preacher, I've come to make you fall. How about it?*"

He said, "*I shook her off like a snake and chased her out of the house.*" He commented, "*Brother Beuttler, just think, if somebody had walked past the house with the door open, and had seen this at the right moment.*"

Whew! My, the risks there are in the ministry! It's an unpleasant subject, and I want to shun it, but I'm not getting away with it.

I was walking along a street in France. I like to go for walks. And I was meandering up toward the central railroad station. All of a sudden, a woman came along and hooked me here in my right arm, gave me a hook - and brother, she could hook! I turned, of course, and knew right away who she was, you understand.

Well, I tried to pull my arm out and couldn't. She had me in a vise. I tried to keep walking, and she walked right with me as though we belonged together. That would never do, you know. I used on her what I have used every so often on men as well as with women (you get it both ways). I used the German equivalent to our "*Enie, menie, minie, mo,*" and rapidly said it in German, and she looked stunned and let go.

I have used that and it has never failed to work, except once with an Arab boy in Algeria. A little shoeshine fellow that pestered me - and they're rascals. Don't you get your shoes shined. Take your own shoeshine business with you if you want to know what's good for you.

"*What's wrong with that?*" you may say.

"You'll find out." An American got his shoes shined in Cairo and the fellow charged him

$5.00.

You'd say, *"Well, I just wouldn't pay."* You'll pay all right, and you'd be glad to. They have a way of making you pay gladly. GLADLY!

That little fellow had liquid shoe polish. He stood back, took the cap off and said, *"Mr. American, would you rather pay me $5.00 or have me throw this liquid shoe polish on your nice suit?"*

He paid $5.00 - gladly. They'll do it. Don't kid yourself.

So with one of those boys is the only time this didn't work. But there in France, I was concerned. I was known there. I thought, *"What if somebody went by in a car or a streetcar and saw us two just at the right moment, me having one of those street women on my arm walking several steps?"*

So in church that afternoon, I said to the people, *"I want to tell you what happened to me in your nice city,"* and I told the whole story just in case some (let's say ladies) didn't go by in a car and say, *"Oh, Oh look, quick look. Did you see it? We saw him with our very own eyes. Would you believe it? What is this world coming to?"* So I told the whole thing.

Of all the things you're up against. *The devil is after the ministry, and you better believe it.*

Let's go back to Samuel. I should have told you that before, but I didn't want to.

"But the Spirit of the Lord departed from Saul, and an evil spirit from the Lord troubled him." I Samuel 16:14.

First of all, I have to try and satisfy you theologians; I mean, you students. "*Now Brother*

Beuttler, what does that mean: An evil spirit from the Lord troubled him?"

I'm not bothering with that, but I'm going to give you what I think, so at least your curiosity is appeased for the present. I think we have two possible explanations. I'll give you both, then I'll give you the one toward which I lean.

1) You can take that to mean that *God deliberately sent an evil spirit to Saul to trouble him.*

2) My personal feeling is that *this spirit was trying to get at Saul right along* (He was the anointed of the Lord.), *but couldn't because of the anointing.* But when God removed His Spirit, the man was open, and God did not intervene. He allowed the spirit the freedom, and in this sense, I think we have these words:

"An evil spirit from the Lord troubled him."

We'd be fools to argue over this, but I personally prefer this latter view.

So now the Spirit of the Lord departed from Saul. *It's*

a terrible thing to lose the presence of God. He lost the presence because of <u>disobedience</u>.

Take Samuel 13:13-14 for instance:

"And Samuel said to Saul, Thou hast done foolishly; *thou hast not kept the commandment of the Lord thy God, which he commanded thee*; for now would the Lord have established thy kingdom upon Israel forever. But now thy kingdom shall not continue; the Lord hath sought him a man after his own heart, and the Lord hath commanded him to be captain over his people, *because thou hast not kept that which the Lord commanded thee*." I Samuel 13:13-14

What happened was the disobedience of Saul. One year, the Lord gave me two definitions: 1) of pride, and 2) of disobedience.

What the Lord gave me for pride was this: <u>*pride is the deification of self, self-deification*</u>. You know, pride is a terrible thing in the sight of God, because <u>when we are proud, we're</u> <u>becoming our own deity, and that infringes on the deity of God.</u>

You have heard or read of Madam Guyon, the French mystic (she's called at least) who knew God so well. She was rated the most beautiful woman in Paris. The men loved to give her a second look. The ladies envied her beauty, and she admired it. But she was a very spiritual woman, and kept seeking the Lord, and realized that her pride of face was hindering her in her spiritual development. She asked the Lord to take away her pride, but her pride go.

One day she challenged God, *"God, do You mean to tell me that You are not strong enough to take this pride out of my heart?"* And the Lord heard it. Madam Guyon came down with smallpox. Her face was full of pox. Her friends told her what salve to use to save her face. She said, *"I'm not using any salve; I'm not saving my face; God is answering my prayer."*

She recovered, but her face was full of marks. Her beauty was gone, but so was her pride. She had no more reason to admire herself in the mirror.

Pride is a terrible thing.

We had a revival in school, and we were coming and going because the revival kept going all the time. I came back to chapel, and sat on one end on the girl's side. I came in and just sat over there.

One of the girls was sitting at the other end of the row of seats - nobody between us, and she was singing in other tongues. It was beautiful. I think she was the greatest singer we ever had. Did that girl have a voice! She could sing way up to K (someplace up there - I'm not a musician though I love music, but know nothing about it.) Did she sing! The chapel was quiet. Everybody was listening to her, and so was I. Oh could that girl sing!

And the Lord spoke to me, *"I want you to go over to Susie* (not her real name), *and tell her that her singing is an abomination in My sight."*

The Manifest Presence of God

Whew!

I said, *"Lord, I can't do that. I have a good relationship with the students, and she has never done anything to me. That's a terrible thing to do."*

A second time He said, *"I want you to go over and tell her that her singing is an abomination in My sight."*

I said, *"God, I can't do that to that girl."* She was one of those nice kids, you know. She'd get cookies from home from her Mom, knock at my door, *"Come in,"* I'd say.

"Brother Beuttler, got some cookies. Would you like some?"

I'd say, *"Sure, I'll take the whole box. How about it?"* You know, that kind of a kid. *"God, and I should tell her that?"* I said. The Lord dealt with me, and I finally

acquiesced. When I wanted to go over, she was gone. Oh, I felt bad. I said, *"Father, forgive me. I'm going to go up to the office, and if You will bring her my way, I will obey."*

I walked up, and down the hall comes Susie. We passed outside my office door. I said, *"Susie, would you mind stepping in my office a moment. I have something to tell you."*

And she said so nicely, *"Certainly, Brother Beuttler,"* in such a nice way. Now I felt all the worse. If she had only demurred, but she was so accommodating.

We went and shut the door. She stood here; I stood there. I looked her in the eye and said nothing. I guess she wondered. I thought, "*Oh brother, that's awfully hard, isn't it?*"

I said, "*Susie, the Lord wants me to tell you that your singing in chapel is an abomination in His sight.*" I said no more. And that girl looked at me as though lightening had struck her.

I could feel her think, "*Brother Beuttler, you, of all people! What have I ever done to you?*" What could I do?

Her head came down and that girl began to weep. She broke out into terrible sobs that I hear for the rest of my life. Oh brother! Her nose started to run, so I gave her my handkerchief. I told you I always have a clean handkerchief in school.

She took it and wept into it. Oh brother! That girl wept. Her whole body heaved. I could have put my arm around that girl's shoulder. I could have and said to her, "*I'm so sorry, what can I do?*" but you can't do that.

There she was, blowing her nose, sobbing. And then she went that way all the way down the hall to the girl's dorm, crying and sobbing the whole way. And I stood outside the door and watched the girl walk down like that.

Whew! What a job this school business is, and <u>*obedience to God*</u>.

She was the favorite singer. She was the soloist; she was in duets, in threeets, in fourets, in fivets, whatever ets there was, she was in it. She sang no more, and to her credit, she never told what happened. Neither did I.

"Susie, will you sing a solo?" "*No,*" she would answer. "*Why not?*"

"*I'm not singing anymore,*" she answered. "*What happened?*"

"*Don't ask me,*" she said.

That girl refused to sing for about three months. I had chapel service, and the Lord laid it upon my heart to ask her to sing a solo. So I looked her up and said, "*Susie, I have chapel tomorrow, and I'd like you to sing a solo for us.*"

She said, "*Me?*" as though saying, "*After what you said, you're asking me?*" (She didn't say that, that's how I felt.) She only said, "*Me?*"

So I said, "*Yes, you.*"

Her head dropped. She paused a bit and said, "*I'll sing.*" And she sang.

School was out very shortly after that. During the summer I received a letter from her:

Dear Brother Beuttler,

I want to thank you for your faithfulness to God and to me for when I was singing in chapel, I was not singing for the glory of the Lord, I was singing to have folk admire my voice. I knew everybody was listening in admiration while I enjoyed their admiration. For some time pride had begun to build up in my heart, and I sang for my own glory. What you said made me realize the state I was in. God humbled me, and broke me, and took the pride out of my heart.

I went to the radio station and asked them to cut for you a 12-inch record on which I'm singing for you your favorite hymns.

Your grateful student, Susie

She came back again the next year and was used again in singing, but her pride was gone.

What a price for <u>obedience</u>!

Saul lost the presence because of <u>*disobedience*</u>, and I almost disobeyed the Lord. Who wants to treat a student that way? And yet, what are you going to do?

I want to go to *the fourth way to lose the presence of the Lord* (*Neglect*) found in Luke 2

You understand, we're dealing here with the principle?

"And when he was twelve years old, they went up to Jerusalem after the custom of the feast. And when they had fulfilled the days, as they returned, the child Jesus tarried behind in Jerusalem; and Joseph and his mother knew not of it. But they, supposing him to have been in the company, went a day's journey; and they sought him among their kinfolk and acquaintance. And when they found him not, they turned back

again to Jerusalem, seeking him. And it came to pass, that after three days they found him in the temple, sitting in the midst of the doctors, both hearing them, and asking them questions." Luke 2:42-46

Now here you have a strange situation:

The most unlikely parents (the parents of Jesus), lost the most unlikely son (the Son of God), in the most unlikely place (the temple), on a most unlikely day (their greatest religious holiday, the Day of Atonement). <u>*The most unlikely people lost the most unlikely son in the most unlikely place on the most unlikely day*</u>. How come?

Sure, they did not want to lose their son. They loved their son, but there's only one answer - *neglect*. They were so *preoccupied* with meeting friends with the holiday season; they noticed his absence, but weren't worried; they *supposed* him to be in the company, but he wasn't. It was a religious holiday, and you'd think on a religious holiday, they wouldn't lose their son, but they did.

That's what happened to me in Bible school. I was in Bible school in 1927, and we had four weeks of special meetings with Brother McGallister. The school was connected with the church, and we had four weeks of meetings. We students were asked to attend classes, do our assignments, be in every service every night, and be at the altar dealing with people. I had wished many a time if I could have told that faculty what a big mistake they made.

I had a wonderful fellowship with God, and it was noticed

by the school and the faculty, and that is the truth. In chapel services, the Lord would give me a message; we'd get an outpouring of the Spirit that even the faculty took notice, *but it came out of my devotional life.*

The four weeks of special meetings robbed me of my relationship with the Lord. There were *too many* classes, *too m*any assignments, *too many* hours with *too much* to do. When the campaign was finished, for me it was a pain in the camp. I had lost what I had before, *because we were so dog-tired.* How could we keep up with the studies and be in church every night and at the altar? And you better be there! It's something I shall never forget, but things were such you couldn't say a word, of course. You simply had to suffer. *It took me a long time to regain what I had lost in those special meetings because the pressures were too great.*

Now here, the parents of Jesus lost their boy, I would say, *through neglect. They did not pay sufficient attention* to their boy, *and after awhile, he was gone.*

One way we can lose the presence of God is through neglect; neglect of the Lord, sacrificing our devotions for study, skipping in our personal devotional life.

How often I had warned in school not to crowd the students with so much studies, assignments and research that we squeeze their devotional life out of them. And I have seen it happen. *We can be so preoccupied*, whether in school or out of school; it's so with ministers; it's so with missionaries. *They get so busy with so many things that this personal relationship suffers, things begin to encroach, and very slowly, the presence begins to subside until it is gone.*

In summary, I would suggest to you tonight *four ways to lose the presence*:

1) **Losing our consecration** - How *jealously* we need to maintain that consecration and not lose the *secret* of the presence of God.

2) **Disobedience** - Now I'll give you the other definition. *Disobedience is the rejection of the throne rights of God.* I think *disobedience is probably the greatest of all sins.*

By the disobedience of one man, all the human race fell; by the obedience of one Christ, the whole human race was saved, that is to say, provision was at least made.

If you can picture God sitting on the throne: *Disobedience is pushing God off His throne and seating ourselves on His throne in His place. Disobedience is the rejection of the throne rights of God.* That's what it is. That's what the Lord gave me, and I think you can see that.

Consequently, *God cannot tolerate disobedience, rebellion against His sovereignty.* As in the case of Saul, *persistence in disobedience will surely rob us of the presence of God.*

3) **Substitution** - Allowing other things to creep into our lives.

When I was in Bible school, I had a girlfriend. The Lord

had warned me against the relationship. The girl was a top girl and students said, "*We sure admire your taste.*" Well, I did too.

Her parents thought that I was everything. In fact, as far as they were concerned, the sun was rising and setting on Beuttler. *But inside the Lord dealt with me not to go through with this thing. The Lord had warned me in a dream.*

In the dream there was a terrible open sore on my shoulder that was draining my life. I looked at it, and woke up, and knew that *this relationship was draining my spiritual life. Nothing was wrong in it, but just the fact of its existence.*

I knelt one night before the Lord and said, "*God, what is wrong with me?*"

And the Lord gave me a scripture right in here (pointing to stomach area), **"Oh that thou hast harkened to my commandments, then would thy peace be like a river."**

It had cost me that wondrous presence of God. I had such a lovely relationship with the

Lord, *but I was taken up now with something else.* And still I wouldn't give in.

We went to New York City to a ten-day evangelistic service with Brother Wigglesworth. She and I were sitting up in the gallery where we had a little privacy. Oh, you don't understand? Well, good for you. They had long benches there, and we were sitting at one corner; she in the corner, I next to her. Wigglesworth was preaching. He stopped, and gave a message in tongues. As he gave the message in tongues, I knew inside instinctively, *"Something is coming for me,"* and it so scared me that I left her sit, and slid up the bench to the other side, and I sat there and let her sit over there. I didn't understand it, but I knew it had to do with her.

Then he came out with the interpretation. And that man came out with exactly what was going on in my heart. And after he got done about submitting to the will of God, he said, *"This message is for a young man in this audience tonight whom God has called."* That did it!

But that continued involvement - and I knew it was out of the will of God - **gradually** *drained me of the presence of God*, and it did not get restored until I had said, *"Sorry, we just can't continue. The Lord just isn't in it."*

<u>How careful we have to be not to let things creep in that are out of harmony to the purpose of the will of God.</u>

4) **Neglect** - *neglecting* our devotion, *neglecting* the Lord, simply being so *preoccupied*

with things that we pay little *attention* to the Lord.

Now in closing, I want to take you to I Chronicles 15.

"And David made him houses in the city of David, and prepared a place for the ark of God, and pitched for it a tent." I Chronicles 15:1

I wish I had an hour for this, but I don't. David was a great lover of the presence of God. *He prepared a place. In making a place for the ark of God, he made a place for the presence, because as you know, the presence of God was there between the cherubim of the ark. David made a place.* Folkses, *we need to be careful to make a place, to make room for the presence in our lives.*

Last night I couldn't get to sleep till at least 1:00 a.m. At 3:00 o'clock, I was awakened with a very heavy presence and Spirit of intercession. Even though I needed sleep so badly (and I'm dreadfully tired tonight because I didn't have enough sleep), I knew it was time to be up and sit in the Lord's presence.

It's a case of *making room* for the presence of God. *Our lives become so cluttered with so many things that little by little the presence of God in our lives becomes displaced through sheer clutter. We need to unclutter our lives; remove a lot of the things that don't matter; that occupy our time, our attention, our hearts, and make room for the presence of God - pitch a tent for it.* <u>The presence of God needs protection against the encroachment of people and things that would disturb it.</u>

Today, I was somewhere around here and had a heavy presence in my spirit, and somebody was going to ask some questions and talk, and I just didn't respond much. *I did not want to be drawn out because I had to put a shield over that intercessory prayer in here* (pointing to stomach).

The Manifest Presence of God

You know, there are *secrets* here that are terrific.

I was going out west one year, and stopped off in Ohio where I saw a schoolmate of mine, Brother Emery. He was our recent president in school. He said to me, "*Oh, I wish I had known you were coming this way. I would have arranged for you to speak. As it is, we have the superintendent.*"

Well I was glad. So we had the meeting. That was all right, and then we had lunch. Brother Emery sat in front of me, and we were chatting. While he talked, *I noticed inside a little presence, not strong, but noticeable. I recognized it as a signal - the Lord attracting my attention. So right away, I spread a tent over it. Now I'm giving you here, a secret of the presence, one of them; the secret of the anointing.*

Instead of talking freely, right away, I cut conversation. I let him do the talking. I cut back with my words to near silence with only a yes and no answer. I did not volunteer; I shielded this presence. And it got stronger. I knew something was up.

Brother Emery kept talking, and he never knew, and doesn't know to this day. *The Lord's presence got stronger, and He dropped a scripture in there*, and the scripture was, **"The Lord will give strength unto His people; the Lord will bless His people with peace,"** and I knew I was going to speak that day. I didn't tell him that. He was the leader, but I didn't tell him.

When I saw that the Lord gave me a scripture, and the thing began to bud and unfold, I said, "*Brother Emery, I wonder if you would be so good and excuse me. I just feel that the Lord would like me to be alone."* That was all right.

I walked into the woods. As I did, this thing grew and grew, and I had a message. I knew

I was going to speak, but the superintendent was scheduled, so I went to the meeting. Brother Emery said, *"Brother Beuttler, come and sit with us."*

"All right," I said and sat with them. It doesn't matter where you sit. They were singing. He was leading. They were singing, singing, singing. I knew they were marking time.

Finally he said, *"Now folks, we have to sing until the superintendent comes."* I thought, *"You'll sing forever. He won't be here."* But I didn't tell him that.

They kept on singing. Then came a telegram, *"Unable to arrive due to circumstances beyond my control."*

Brother Emery said, *"I'm awfully sorry. Here is the telegram. Now we're stuck for a preacher. What are we going to do?"*

I said not a word. Oh no!

He said, *"Well, my schoolmate from CBI is here. Brother Beuttler, do you think you could perhaps give us a little testimony?"*

I said, *"Oh, I think so."*

I'm not exaggerating, I turned to my scripture in Psalms 29 and read it, and the message flowed out like it were dipped in oil for about an hour and a quarter; just flowed; the glory came down; hands went up. We had a wonderful meeting, *BUT I had covered the presence. David spread a covering over the presence. We need to shield the presence of God against the encroachment of things.*

As you know, *we have a wonderful treasure in the presence of God, but it can be lost through lack of consecration, disobedience, substitution and neglect.*

May I say that *in all we do, let's be sure we make room for the presence of God in our lives, moving aside the clutter, the things that don't matter, that there might be room for the presence. And having the presence, spreading a tent over it, protecting the presence of God against the encroachment of things which would dissipate and cause it to be lost.*

I trust the Lord will be able to say to you as well as to me, **"My presence shall go with thee, and I will give thee rest."**

Thank you very much for the privilege of being with you. It was a treat, not a treatment.

Afterword

Here is a short story from a Pentecostal bible school in Pennsylvania that had this account of Walter's visit to their school:

In memory of Walter Beuttler who went beyond seeking God for His blessings but sought God for Himself.

The student body of Western Pennsylvania Bible Institute was abuzz. Walter Beuttler was coming next week to speak to us. I had never heard Walter speak so I really didn't know what to expect. I thought to myself though that he must be some speaker to have the older students so excited. There weren't to many speakers they were excited about because they had heard so many.

The day finally arrived. The church was packed. Not only with students, but people had driven for miles to be at chapel that day. I thought to myself that this guy must be something to cause such excitement. What kind of preacher is he? Maybe he's a jumping jack like one of my favorite preachers Jumping Jack Stewart? Perhaps his voice thunders like Jim Salvador when he gets excited in the Lord? Maybe he's bouncy and funny like Mac McClure who I always loved to hear preach when I was a boy? Wonder if he plays the guitar and sings like Mike McCracken does?

What's special about this guy that's causing such an excitement?

When Walter walked into the chapel with Hubert Bunney that day I thought to myself, "He's an ordinary looking guy. Nice suit, shiny shoes, old. Wonder what the fuss is about?"

I looked toward the platform and noticed a desk and a swivel chair. I couldn't remember ever seeing a desk and a chair on a platform before especially in a Pentecostal service.

We sang a bit. It was good but it seemed that we were somewhat distracted that morning. I realized what it was. Everyone who knew him was anxious to hear from Walter. Finally Brother Bunney introduced him and he slowly walked to the platform and sat down in the swivel chair. I thought to myself, "This is interesting. Never saw this before. The chandeliers are safe."

He had us turn our Bibles to Acts 14:26-28 and began to tell us stories. Stories? I thought to myself. And the way he told them he wasn't even that great of a storyteller. He spoke slowly with not a whole lot of variation in his voice. I scanned the church to see the reaction of others. Were they as disappointed as I was becoming? They didn't seem to be. They listened very intently as if in anticipation. What were they expecting I thought? I decided to listen closer.

The Manifest Presence of God

As I listened to him I began to hear something a little different then what I was used to. When he talked about Jesus he didn't just pump out information about Him. He talked about Jesus as though he were his friend. This got my attention and I started to listen more intently. I realized that the stories were a little more than stories. They were stories about adventures that he'd had with his friend Jesus.

He traveled the world teaching about his friend. He told us that he usually traveled alone, but not alone, because of the companionship of the presence of God. I listened as he told of the time he and Jesus were flying over the Atlantic together on their way to London. They were having a good time when Jesus said to him, "I'll meet you beside the pyramids Walter." And then it seemed like the Lord took off. When Walter landed in London he bought a ticket to Egypt, arrived there, went to the pyramids and sat down. When he sat down he sensed the presence of his friend. Shortly an Egyptian businessman came and sat down beside them. Walter knew that he was the reason the Lord wanted to come to Egypt. It wasn't long until Walter began talking to him about his friend and the Egyptian asked if the Lord would be his friend too. Walter told him that Jesus wanted to be his friend, introduced him to Jesus, then got back on a plane and resumed his trip. He and his friend.

Walter told us of several adventures that he'd had with his friend that day. I'll never forget this one he told. When he arrived in Bangkok he discovered that his baggage had been lost. He decided to go to the motel and wait until he received a call saying that his baggage had arrived. No such call came so he decided to go back to the airport and go to the conveyor belt to check. Nothing. He'd pretty much reconciled himself to the fact that his baggage was lost and figured on buying replacements. As he turned to leave the conveyor belt suddenly he felt the presence of the Lord. It seemed to him that the Lord didn't want to leave the conveyor belt. Walter thought to himself that if the Lord wanted to stay at the conveyor belt he should too. Walter began to appreciate the presence of his friend and began to worship him. He got caught up in worship when suddenly his luggage appeared on the belt. It had gotten mixed up with the luggage of another flight.

When Walter finished telling us stories about his friend that day he did an interesting thing. He slowly turned his back to the congregation. And just waited. I thought, I haven't seen this before. No one moved. A holy hush took over. There was total silence for several moments when suddenly a woman stood crying. She began to confess sins to the whole church. I couldn't believe it. Walter? He just continued to wait with his back to the congregation until she was finished. No sooner had she finished and someone else stood and began to confess their sins to the church. Person after person stood.

Eventually I stood as well. The presence of God was electrifying. It was serious. Compassionate. Loving. All that! When finally things quieted down again Walter Beuttler turned back to the congregation and thanked us for loving his friend and walked off the platform."

Deeper Life Press
Refuge Ministries
P.O Box 381
Bloomfield, NY 14469

*For free audio and written messages as well as other resources from Walter Beuttler please visit our online library at www.findrefuge.tv